# Data Structures and Algorithms in Swift

## Implement Stacks, Queues, Dictionaries, and Lists in Your Apps

Elshad Karimov

Apress®

*Data Structures and Algorithms in Swift: Implement Stacks, Queues, Dictionaries, and Lists in Your Apps*

Elshad Karimov
New York, New York, USA

ISBN-13 (pbk): 978-1-4842-5768-5          ISBN-13 (electronic): 978-1-4842-5769-2
https://doi.org/10.1007/978-1-4842-5769-2

Managing Director, Apress Media LLC: Welmoed Spahr
Acquisitions Editor: Aaron Black
Development Editor: James Markham
Coordinating Editor: Jessica Vakili

Distributed to the book trade worldwide by Springer Science+Business Media New York, 233 Spring Street, 6th Floor, New York, NY 10013. Phone 1-800-SPRINGER, fax (201) 348-4505, e-mail orders-ny@springer-sbm.com, or visit www.springeronline.com. Apress Media, LLC is a California LLC and the sole member (owner) is Springer Science + Business Media Finance Inc (SSBM Finance Inc). SSBM Finance Inc is a **Delaware** corporation.

For information on translations, please e-mail rights@apress.com, or visit http://www.apress.com/rights-permissions.

Apress titles may be purchased in bulk for academic, corporate, or promotional use. eBook versions and licenses are also available for most titles. For more information, reference our Print and eBook Bulk Sales web page at http://www.apress.com/bulk-sales.

Any source code or other supplementary material referenced by the author in this book is available to readers on GitHub via the book's product page, located at www.apress.com/978-1-4842-5768-5. For more detailed information, please visit http://www.apress.com/source-code.

Printed on acid-free paper

# Table of Contents

# About the Author

**Elshad Karimov** is an experienced programmer with more than 8 years experience of different programming languages and a solid background in iOS development as well as Oracle, SQL, C#, Java, Python and HTML/CSS. He's familiar with the performance limits and characteristics of Swift and the nature and function of embedded databases and system datastores.

# About the Technical Reviewer

**Felipe Laso** is a Senior Systems Engineer working at Lextech Global Services. He's also an aspiring game designer/programmer. You can follow him on Twitter @iFeliLM or on his blog.

# CHAPTER 1

# Arrays

In this chapter, you will learn about arrays, their built-in properties, and how to retrieve, add, and remove elements from them.

## Introduction

An array is simply a container that can hold multiple data (values) of any data type in an ordered list; this means that you get the elements in the same order as you defined the items in the array. Instead of declaring individual variables, such as number0, number1, and so on … until number99, you declare one array variable such as numbers and use numbers[0], numbers[1], and numbers[99] to represent individual variables.

The simplest type of array is the linear array, which is also known as a one-dimensional array. In Swift, arrays are a zero-based index. A one-dimensional array can be written simply as shown in the following and elements can be accessed using a[i], where i is an index between 0 and n:

$$a = \begin{bmatrix} a_0 \\ a_1 \\ \vdots \\ a_n \end{bmatrix}$$

© Elshad Karimov 2020
E. Karimov, *Data Structures and Algorithms in Swift*,
https://doi.org/10.1007/978-1-4842-5769-2_1

Another form of array is the multidimensional array which is a typical matrix:

$$a = \begin{bmatrix} a_{00} & a_{01} & a_{02} \\ a_{10} & a_{11} & a_{12} \end{bmatrix}$$

# Main Features of Arrays

Each element can be accessed through its index, as shown in Figure 1-1.

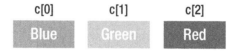

***Figure 1-1.*** *Element index*

Arrays reserve a specific capacity of memory for holding their contents, and when the capacity is full, the array allocates a larger region of memory for additional elements and copies its elements into the new storage. This is why adding elements to an array can be time consuming. The new storage size grows exponentially as compared to the old size, so as the array grows, reallocation occurs less and less often. The capacity property determines the total amount of elements the array can contain before exceeding and having to allocate new memory.

As shown in Figure 1-2, we're appending "Black" to the array that's just about to exceed its capacity. The item doesn't get added right away, but what happens is new memory is created elsewhere, all items are copied over, and finally the item is added to the array. This is called reallocation: allocating new storage at another region in memory. The array's size increases exponentially. In Swift, this is called the geometric growth pattern.

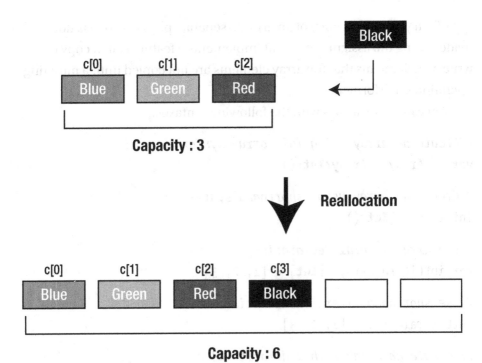

**Figure 1-2.** *Reallocation*

As the elements are added to an array, the array will automatically resize when it runs out of capacity. It is more efficient to allocate additional reserve capacity at creation time if you know ahead of time an array will contain a large number of elements.

```
var intArray = Array<Int>()

//Shows the array capacity
intArray.capacity
intArray.reserveCapacity(500)
intArray.capacity
```

3

When you make a copy of an array, a separate physical copy is not made during the assignment. Swift implements a feature called copy on write, which means that the array elements are not copied until a mutating operation is performed.

You can create arrays with the following syntaxes:

```
//Create an array using full array syntax
var intArray = Array<Int>()
```

```
//Create an array using shorthand syntax
intArray = [Int]()
```

```
//Use array literal declaration
var intLiteralArray: [Int] = [1, 2, 3]
```

```
//Use shorthand literal declaration
intLiteralArray = [1, 2, 3]
```

```
// Create an array with a default value
intLiteralArray = [Int](repeating: 2, count: 5)
```

# Retrieving Elements from an Array

There are multiple ways to retrieve values from an array. We can retrieve using index or loop through using the for-in syntax.

```
var myIntArray = [1,2,3,4,5]
var aNumber = myIntArray[2]
print(aNumber)
```

```
//Output
3
```

We can iterate through the elements in an array.

```
for element in myIntArray {
    print(element)
}

//Output
1
2
3
4
5
```

# Adding Elements to an Array

There are two ways of adding an element to an array. Append function can be used to add an element at the end of the array and insert function can be used to insert an element at a specific index in an existing array.

```
myIntArray.append(11)
print(myIntArray)

//Output
[1, 2, 3, 4, 5, 11]

myIntArray.insert(12, at: 3)
print(myIntArray)

//Output
[1, 2, 3, 12, 4, 5, 11]
```

# Removing Elements from an Array

Similarly, there are four ways of removing elements from an array. By using removeLast() function, an element at the end of an array can be removed, removeFirst() to remove the first element, remove(at:) to remove an element at a specific index, and removeAll() to remove all elements.

```
myIntArray.removeLast()
myIntArray.removeFirst()
myIntArray.remove(at: 1)
myIntArray.removeAll()
```

# Built-in Functions and Properties

In the remaining sections, we'll discuss some built-in functions and properties of arrays.

## isEmpty

This property determines if an array is empty or not. It returns true if an array does not contain any value, otherwise returns false.

```
let myIntArray = [1, 3, 5, 6]
print(myIntArray.isEmpty)
```

When you run the program, the output will be

```
false
```

# First and Last

These properties are used to access the first and last elements of an array.

```
print(myIntArray.first)
print(myIntArray.last)
```

When you run the program, the output will be

**Optional**(1)
**Optional**(6)

As you can see, the output of these properties is optional. This means that if the array is empty the return will be nil.

# Reversed and Reverse

Reversed function returns completely new collection with the elements of an array in reverse order. Reverse function reverses the collection itself.

```
let reversedArray = Array(myIntArray.reversed())
print(reversedArray)
```

When you run the program, the output will be

```
[6, 5, 3, 1]
```

# Count

This property returns the total number of elements in an array.

```
print(myIntArray.count)
```

When you run the program, the output will be

4

## Important

While using subscript syntax to access elements of an array in Swift, you must be sure the value lies in the index; otherwise, you will get a runtime crash. Let's see this in the following example:

```
print(myIntArray[-1])
```

When you run the program, the output will be

```
fatal error: Index out of range
```

In the preceding program, there is no value in the index **-1**. So when you try to access the value in the index, you will get a runtime crash.

To prevent this, first find the index of the element you are trying to remove. And then remove the element at the index as follows:

```
var myIntArray = [1, 3, 5, 7]
if let index = myIntArray.firstIndex(of: 5) {
    print("found index")
    let val =  myIntArray.remove(at: index)
    print(val)
}
```

When you run the program, the output will be

```
found index
5
```

## Conclusion

In this chapter, you have learned about the general structure of an array, how to declare it in Swift, and how to select, add, and remove elements. In the following chapter, you will learn about the data structure type of dictionaries.

# CHAPTER 2

# Dictionaries

In this chapter, the dictionary type of data structures will be discussed. You will learn how to access, add, remove, and modify elements in a dictionary. Moreover, built-in properties and functions of dictionaries will be covered.

## Introduction

A dictionary is another data type collection in Swift. This data structure takes its name from real-world dictionaries where you have words and their associated meaning; in programming, we use dictionaries to associate a key with its value, so any value can be identified as long as we know the key. If we look inside a real dictionary, we will find words and each word has accompanying explanation and meaning.

Miller : a person who owns or works in a corn mill

There is a similar concept in Swift, in which we can express the preceding dictionary entry like this where a key is a word from a real dictionary and the value is an accompanying explanation.

```swift
var myDict = ["Miller" : "a person who owns or works in a corn mill"]
```

It is an unordered collection that holds multiple data as key/value pair. Each value is associated with a unique key that acts as an identifier for the value in the dictionary. A key is used to store and retrieve values from the dictionary.

© Elshad Karimov 2020
E. Karimov, *Data Structures and Algorithms in Swift*,
https://doi.org/10.1007/978-1-4842-5769-2_2

```
var myDict = ["Miller" : "a person who owns or works in a corn mill",
              "Programmer" : "a person who writes computer programs"]
```

We can add more than one key to the dictionary as long as it conforms to the declaration of the dictionary. We can create dictionaries by explicitly stating how the data is structured in a dictionary. In this, case we have the key String data type and the value is also a String data type. If we state the dictionary structure, the declaration will be like this:

```
var myDict : [String : String] = ["Miller" : "a person who owns
                                              or works in a corn mill",
                                   "Programmer" : "a person who
                                              writes computer programs"]
```

Suppose you may want to search the capital city of a country. In that case, you will create a dictionary with the key country and value capital city. Now, you get the capital city from the collection by searching with the key country. If we want to create a dictionary with different types of values, we need to declare a heterogeneous dictionary which conforms to the Hashable protocol. This type of dictionaries is useful when converting JSON payloads.

```
var myDictionary = [AnyHashable: Any]()
```

There are three ways of dictionary declaration:

```
// 1St
var myDictionary = Dictionary<Int, String>()

// 2nd
var myDictionary = [Int: String]()

// 3rd
var myDictionary:[Int: String] = [:]
```

It is possible to create a dictionary from two arrays:

```
let countryKeys = ["US", "UK", "AZ"]
let countryValues = ["United States", "United Kingdom",
                     "Azerbaijan"]
let newDictionary = Dictionary(uniqueKeysWithValues:
                     zip(countryKeys,countryValues))
print(newDictionary)
```

When you run the program, the output will be

**["AZ": "Azerbaijan", "US": "United States", "UK": "United Kingdom"]**

# Accessing Values in a Dictionary

To access any value in a dictionary, you need to include the key of the value you want to access within square brackets immediately after the name of the dictionary. It is possible to use optional binding and forced unwrapping or determine if the value exists to retrieve the pair. If you are absolutely sure that the key exists, only then in this case forced unwrapping can be used.

Using optional binding

```
//Using optional binding
var myDictionary : [Int: String] = [1: "One", 2: "Two", 3: "Three"]
if let optValue = myDictionary[4] {
    print(optValue)
} else {
    print("Key not found")
}
```

The output will be

**Key** not found

Using forced unwrapping

```
//Using forced unwrapping
let forcedValue = myDictionary[3]!
print(forcedValue)
```

The output will be

**Three**

It is possible to iterate through a dictionary and return the key pair, which can be decomposed into named constants.

```
for (key, value) in myDictionary {
    print("The value for \(key) is \(value)")
}
```

The output will be **key: 3**

**The value for 1 is One**
**The value for 2 is Two**
**The value for 3 is Three**

It is possible to retrieve only the keys or values independently. As mentioned before, dictionaries are unordered collections, so when you iterate through them, there is no guarantee that it will be listed in an order. But there might be occasions that you want an iteration in an ordered manner, and for those cases, sort(_:) method can be used. This will return an array containing sorted elements of a dictionary. In the following code, $0.0 is the first key/value pair and $0.1 is the second key/value pair. These pairs are compared and will be ordered based on this comparison. Then, a map method is used to retrieve the data for the key or value.

```
let sortedArray = myDictionary.sorted(by: {$0.0 < $1.0})

for (key) in sortedArray.map({$0.0}) {
    print("The key: \(key)")
}

for (value) in sortedArray.map({$0.1}) {
    print("The value: \(value)")
}
```

The output will be

```
The key: 1
The key: 2
The key: 3
The value: One
The value: Three
The value: Four
```

# Adding/Modifying to a Dictionary

To add a value to a dictionary, a subscript notation or
updateValue(_:forKey) method can be used. The subscript notation can
also be used to modify any existing value.

```
// Add a new element to the dictionary
myDictionary.updateValue("Four", forKey: 4)
```

```
//Add a new element using subscript notation
myDictionary[5] = "Five"
```

# Removing a Value from a Dictionary

To remove a value from a dictionary, a subscript notation and removeValue(forKey:) method can be used. This method returns the value that was removed.

```
//Remove a value from a dictionary using the method
let removedValue = myDictionary.removeValue(forKey: 1)

//Remove a value using subscript notation
myDictionary[2] = nil
```

# Built-in Functions and Properties
## isEmpty

It returns true if a dictionary does not contain any value, otherwise returns false.

```
print(myDictionary.isEmpty)
```

The output will be

```
false
```

# First

This property is used to access the first element of a dictionary.

```
let myDictionary : [Int: String] = [1: "One", 2: "Two",
3: "Three"]

print(myDictionary.first)
```

The output will be

```
Optional((key: 2, value: "Two"))
```

# Count

It returns the total number of elements in a dictionary.

```
print(myDictionary.count)
```

The output will be

```
3
```

# Keys

It returns all the keys inside a dictionary.

```
let dictKeys  = Array(myDictionary.keys)
print(dictKeys)
```

The output will be

```
[1,2,3]
```

# Conclusion

In this chapter, you have learned about the structure of dictionaries and how to access, add, remove, and modify elements in it. The built-in properties and functions provided by the Swift programming language are also covered.

# CHAPTER 3

# Sets

It is an unordered collection (meaning you won't get the elements in the same order as you defined) of unique, non-nil elements. It must conform to the **Hashable** protocol. This means it has to provide a hashValue property. This is important because sets are unordered and hashValue is used to access the elements of the sets.

Access time is more efficient than arrays. When searching for an element inside an array, the worst scenario is **O(n)**, where n is the size of the array, but in a set, it is always constant **O(1)**. Unlike other collection types while declaring sets, a set type must be specified.

```
//Full syntax declaration
var intSet = Set<Int>()

//Initialize a set from an array literal
var stringSet: Set = ["One", "Two", "Three"]
```

## Accessing, Adding, and Removing an Element of a Set

## Accessing an Element

As previously mentioned, sets are unordered and do not have indexes, so it is not possible to access elements of a set using **subscript** syntax as arrays. It can be accessed through using the set's own methods and properties or using for-in loops.

© Elshad Karimov 2020
E. Karimov, *Data Structures and Algorithms in Swift*,
https://doi.org/10.1007/978-1-4842-5769-2_3

```
// Accessing an element
for num in stringSet {
    print(num)
}
```

The output will be

**Two**
**One**
**Three**

For ordered iteration, the following method can be used:

```
//Ordered iteration
for num in stringSet.sorted() {
    print(num)
}
```

To check if an element exists in a set, contains(_:) method can be used.

```
// Check if the element exists
if stringSet.contains("One") {
    print("Element found")
} else {
    print("Element not found")
}
```

The output will be

**Element found**

# Adding an Element

Using the insert() method, a new element can be added to a set.

```
//Insert a new element
stringSet.insert("Four")
print(stringSet)
```

The output will be

**["Four", "One", "Two", "Three"]**

# Removing Elements

There are several methods that can be used to remove the elements from a set.

> remove(_:) - To remove an element when you have an instance of it
>
> remove(at:) - To remove the element when you know the index
>
> removeFirst() - To remove the first element and starting index
>
> removeAll() or removeAll(keepCapacity) - To remove all elements

```
//Remove an element
stringSet.remove("Four")
```

```
//Remove an element in an index
if let idx = stringSet.firstIndex(of: "One") {
    stringSet.remove(at: idx)
}
```

```
// Remove first
stringSet.removeFirst()
```

```
//Remove all
stringSet.removeAll()
```

# Set Operations

One of the main advantages of using sets is you can perform two types of set operations – comparison operations and membership and equality operations. These are similar to the set operations in Math.

# Comparison Operations

There are four methods for performing comparison operations in Swift: union, intersection, subtracting, and symmetric difference. Let's review them now.

## Union

The union of two sets is the set of all values from both sets (Figure 3-1).

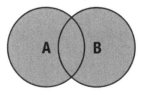

***Figure 3-1.*** *Union of two sets*

The union(_:) and formUnion(_:) methods are used to unite two sets which create a new set with all values from both sets. The second function deletes all elements from the first set (**A**) and inserts the union of **A** and **B**, which means that you cannot use this function when you declare set with as constant set with **let** keyword; to use the formUnion(_:) method, first set A must be declared with **var** keyword.

```
//Union
let A: Set = [1, 3, 5, 7]
let B: Set = [0, 2, 4, 6]
print(A.union(B))
```

The output will be

```
[3, 6, 2, 0, 7, 5, 1, 4]
```

## Intersection

The intersection of two sets is the set with elements only common to both (Figure 3-2).

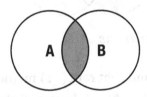

*Figure 3-2. Intersection of two sets*

The intersection(_:) and formIntersection(_:) methods are used to intersect two sets which creates a new set from the common elements of both sets. The second function deletes all elements from the first set (**A**) and inserts the intersection of **A** and **B**, which means that you cannot use this function when you declare set with as constant set with **let** keyword; to use the formIntersection(_:) method, first set **A** must be declared as a variable using the **var** keyword.

```
//Intersection
let A: Set = [1, 2, 3, 4, 5]
let B: Set = [0, 2, 4, 6, 8]
print(A.intersection(B))
```

The output will be

**[2, 4]**

## Subtracting

The subtracting of two sets is the set that contains all elements from the first set except the ones which belong to the second set (Figure 3-3).

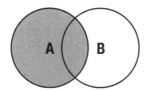

***Figure 3-3.*** *Subtracting two sets*

The subtracting(_:) and subtract(_:) methods are used for subtracting of two sets. subtract(_:) deletes all elements from the first set (**A**) and inserts the subtraction of **A** and **B**, which means that you cannot use this function when you declare set with as constant set with **let** keyword; to use this method, first set **A** must be declared as a variable using the **var** keyword.

```
//Subtracting
var A: Set = [1, 3, 5, 7, 9]
let B: Set = [0, 3, 7, 6, 8]
print(A.subtracting(B))
```

The output will be

**[1, 5, 9]**

# Symmetric Difference

The symmetric difference of two sets is the set that contains all elements from both sets except the common ones (Figure 3-4).

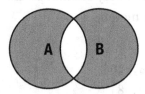

***Figure 3-4.*** *Symmetric difference of two sets*

The symmetricDifference(_:) and formSymmetricDifference(_:) methods are used for the symmetric difference of two sets. The same principles apply here to use the second function; first, the set must be declared as a variable, and this method, (formSymmetricDifference(_:)), deletes all elements from the first set (A) and inserts the symmetric difference of both sets.

```
//Symmetric difference
var A: Set = [1, 2, 3, 4, 5]
var B: Set = [0, 2, 4, 6, 8]
print(A.symmetricDifference(B))
```

The output will be

```
[5, 1, 6, 3, 0, 8]
```

# Membership and Equality Operations

## Set Equality

Two sets are said to be equal if they contain precisely the same values and the order of values does not matter.

```
//Set equality
let A: Set = [2, 4, 6, 8, 10]
let B: Set = [0, 3, 7, 6, 8]
let C: Set = [10, 8, 4, 2, 6]

if A == B {
    print("A and B are equal")
} else {
    print("A and B are different")
}

if A == C {
    print("A and C are equal")
} else {
    print("A and C are different")
}
```

The output will be

```
A and B are different
A and C are equal
```

# Set Membership

Using the set membership methods, the relationship between the two sets can be identified.

isSubset(of:) – Use this method to determine if all of the values of a set are contained in a specified set.

isStrictSubset(of:) – Use this method to determine if a set is a subset, but not equal to the specified set.

isSuperset(of:) – Use this method to determine if a set contains all of the values of the specified set.

isStrictSuperset(of:) – Use this method to determine if a set is a superset, but not equal to the specified set.

isDisjoint(with:) – Use this method to determine if the two have the same values in common.

```
//Set membership
let A: Set = [2, 4, 6, 8, 10]
let B: Set = [0, 4, 2, 6, 7, 9, 10, 8]

print("isSubset:", A.isSubset(of: B))
print("isSuperset:", B.isSuperset(of: A))
print("isStrictSubset:", A.isStrictSubset(of: B))
print("isDisjointWith:", A.isDisjoint(with: B))
```

The output will be

**isSubset: true**
**isSuperset: true**
**isStrictSubset: true**
**isDisjointWith: false**

isSubset returns true because set **B** contains all the elements in **A**.

isSuperset returns true because set **B** contains all of the values of **A**.

isStrictSubset returns true because set **B** contains all the element in **A** and both sets are not equal.

`isDisjointWith` returns `false` because sets **A** and **B** have some values in common.

## Conclusion

In this chapter, you have learned about the general structure of sets, how to declare them in Swift, and how to select, add, and remove elements and set operations such as union, intersection, subtracting, and symmetric difference. In the following chapter, you will learn about the data structure type of Stack.

# CHAPTER 4

# Stacks

A stack is a **last in first out (LIFO)** data structure. The structure of a stack can be imagined as a pile of objects stacked vertically (Figure 4-1). When extracting these objects, the last added to the stack is the first one removed. Stacks are similar to arrays but with limited control.

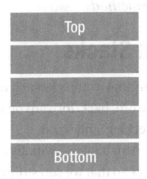

***Figure 4-1.*** *Stack structure*

There are three methods that stacks implement. By using push() method, a new element can be added to the top of the stack, pop() method to remove an element from the top, and peek() method to return the top element from the stack without removing it (Figure 4-2).

© Elshad Karimov 2020
E. Karimov, *Data Structures and Algorithms in Swift*,
https://doi.org/10.1007/978-1-4842-5769-2_4

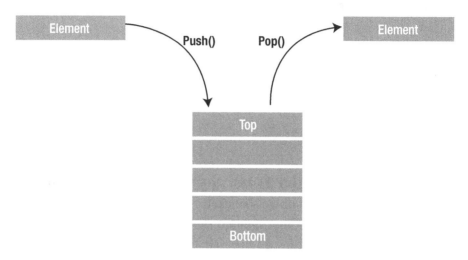

***Figure 4-2.*** *Stack's three methods*

# Using Swift with Stacks

There are many applications that use stacks such as Undo/Redo stacks in Excel or Word, reversing a word, back/forward on browsers, backtracking algorithms, parenthesis checking, and so on.

Let's continue to implement it using Swift. By using Swift Generics, we provide flexibility to the stack so that we can store any type. First, we create a Stack structure and declare the private array type of Swift Generics with an empty array. This items array will be used to hold our Stack's values.

```
import Foundation

public struct Stack<T> {
    private var items: [T] = []
}
```

Then we will continue to write three methods that are required in Stacks. First we will create the push() function.

```
import Foundation

public struct Stack<T> {
    private var items: [T] = []

    //Push method
    mutating func push(element: T) {
        items.append(element)
    }
}
```

Basically, what we are doing here is to append items by adding an element to the top of the array. The mutating keyword is used to allow the method to modify the data contained in the structure. Notice that a push operation puts the new element at the end of the array, not at the beginning. Inserting at the beginning of an array is expensive, an **O(n)** operation, because it requires all existing array elements to be shifted in memory. Adding at the end is **O(1)**; it always takes the same amount of time, regardless of the size of the array.

Then we will write the pop() method which is responsible to extract the data from the Stack.

```
import Foundation

public struct Stack<T> {
    private var items: [T] = []

    //Push method
    mutating func push(element: T) {
        items.append(element)
    }
```

```
    //Pop method
    mutating func pop() -> T? {
        return items.popLast()
    }
}
```

The arrays provide a popLast() method to remove the topmost element from the array and it returns optional, and this differs popLast() from removeLast(), so this is why we declared the return type as an optional **T?**.

The only method that is left is the peek() function. It returns the top element of the Stack.

```
import Foundation

public struct Stack<T> {
    private var items: [T] = []

    //Push method
    mutating func push(element: T) {
        items.append(element)
    }

    //Pop method
    mutating func pop() -> T? {
        return items.popLast()
    }

    //Peek method
    func peek() -> T? {
        return items.last
    }
}
```

# Stack Structures

Let's take a look at the examples of how we can use our stack structure.

```
var customStack = Stack<Int>()

//Using push method
customStack.push(element: 4)
print(customStack)
customStack.push(element: 8)
print(customStack)
customStack.push(element: 12)
print(customStack)

//Using peek method
print(customStack.peek()!)

//Using pop method
var x = customStack.pop()
print(x!)
x = customStack.pop()
print(x!)
```

The output will be

```
Stack<Int>(items: [4])
Stack<Int>(items: [4, 8])
Stack<Int>(items: [4, 8, 12])

    12

    12
    8
```

Basically, we are creating customStack using the Stack structure with integer type and using the push() method inserting new elements at the top of the Stack. Every time after insertion, we print the Stack to the console to see the order of the elements that are inserted into the stack, and it is clear that it inserts at the top. Then we use the peek() method and print the value to the console; it can be easily seen that the top last element of the array is returned. Finally, we use the pop() method to remove the top value and return it, and it is obvious that when you run it a second time, it will return the next element as the top one is removed.

# Stack Extensions

We can add extensions to the Stack to extend its behavior and functionality. There are many extensions such as **CustomStringConvertible**, **ExpressibleByArrayLiteral**, **IteratorProtocol**, **Sequence** protocol, and so on that can be added to the stack for more functionalities. By adding **CustomStringConvertible** protocol, we can change the printout as the way we want.

```
extension Stack: CustomStringConvertible {
    public var description: String {
        return items.description
    }
}
```

# Conclusion

In this chapter, you have learned about the general structure of Stacks, how to create them in Swift, and how to use push, pop, and peek methods and stack extensions. In the following chapter, you will learn about the data structure type of queue.

# CHAPTER 5

# Queue

A queue is a first in first out (FIFO) data structure which means first come first serve. It is also known as "waiting lines," and as the name suggests, it can be easily imagined as a group of people waiting in a line (Figure 5-1).

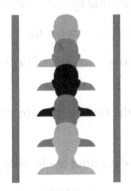

***Figure 5-1.*** *Typical queue structure*

When a new person comes, he stands at the end of the line conveniently adding data to a queue; the data is placed at the end. The term "enqueue" is used to refer to the act of adding an element to a queue. When extracting data from a queue, the data that has been in the queue the longest is removed first – the term "dequeue" refers to the act of extracting data from a queue (Figure 5-2).

© Elshad Karimov 2020
E. Karimov, *Data Structures and Algorithms in Swift,*
https://doi.org/10.1007/978-1-4842-5769-2_5

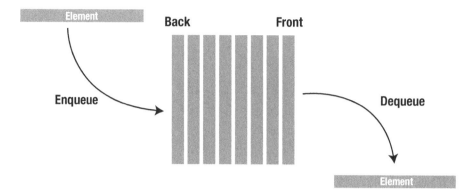

***Figure 5-2.*** *Enqueue/dequeue example*

There are several methods that queues implement.

enqueue() – Add an element at the end of the queue

dequeue() – Remove and return the first element from the queue

peek() – Return the first element from the queue, but not remove it

count – Return the number of elements in the queue

clear() – Reset the queue to an empty state

isEmpty() – Return true if the queue is empty

isFull() : Return true if the queue if full

Queue, as the name suggests, is used whenever we need to manage any group of objects in an order in which the first one coming in also gets out first, while the others wait for their turn, like in the following scenarios:

1.  Point of sale system of a restaurant. It is obvious that the orders must be processed in the order they were received. As an order is received, it writes to the back of the queue and reads orders from the front of the queue by cooks' device. This allows cooks to cook meals in the order they received.

2. Serving requests on a single shared resource, like a printer, CPU task scheduling, and so on.

3. In a real-life scenario, call center phone systems use queues to hold people calling them in an order, until a service representative is free.

4. Handling of interrupts in real-time systems. The interrupts are handled in the same order as they arrive.

5. Buffers on MP3 players and portable CD players and iPod playlist. Playlist for jukebox – add songs to the end, and play from the front of the list.

6. When programming a real-time system that can be interrupted (e.g., by a mouse click or wireless connection), it is necessary to attend to the interrupts immediately before proceeding with the current activity. If the interrupts should be handled in the same order they arrive, then a FIFO queue is the appropriate data structure.

# Implementation

By using Swift Generics, we provide flexibility to the queue so that we can store any type. First, we will create a queue structure and declare the private array type of Swift Generics with an empty array of **T** type.

```swift
import Foundation

public struct Queue<T> {
    private var data: [T] = []
}
```

Then we will add the enqueue() method which appends new element to the end of the queue, and again here, the time complexity will be **O(1).**

```
import Foundation

public struct Queue<T> {
    private var data: [T] = []

    //Enqueue method
    public mutating func enqueue(element: T) {
        data.append(element)
    }
}
```

We continue to declare the **dequeue**() method which removes and returns the first element in the queue, and if the queue is empty, it returns nil.

```
import Foundation

public struct Queue<T> {
    private var data: [T] = []

    //Enqueue method
    public mutating func enqueue(element: T) {
        data.append(element)
    }

    //Dequeue method
    public mutating func dequeue() -> T? {
        return data.removeFirst()
    }
}
```

Another method that can be used is the peek() function which returns the first element in the queue without removing it, and again if it is empty, nil is returned.

```
public struct Queue<T> {
    private var data: [T] = []

    //Enqueue method
    public mutating func enqueue(element: T) {
        data.append(element)
    }

    //Dequeue method
    public mutating func dequeue() -> T? {
        return data.removeFirst()
    }

    //Peek method
    public func peek() -> T? {
        return data.first
    }
}
```

We can even go further to declare the helper functions that are previously mentioned. The full code for the helper functions will be as follows – count, clear(), isEmpty(), and isFull():

```
import Foundation

public struct Queue<T> {
    private var data: [T] = []

    //Enqueue method
    public mutating func enqueue(element: T) {
        data.append(element)
    }
```

```swift
//Dequeue method
public mutating func dequeue() -> T? {
    return data.removeFirst()
}

//Peek method
public func peek() -> T? {
    return data.first
}

// Clear
public mutating func clear() {
    data.removeAll()
}

//Count
public var count: Int {
    return data.count
}

//Capacity will be used for isFull() method
public var capacity: Int {
    get {
        return data.capacity
    }
    set {
        data.reserveCapacity(newValue)
    }
}

//isFull method
public func isFull() -> Bool {
    return count == data.capacity
}
```

```
//isEmpty() method
public func isEmpty() -> Bool {
    return data.isEmpty
}
}
```

The following code and Figure 5-3 illustrate a real-life example of using the queue methods:

```
var cusTomQueue = Queue<Int>()

cusTomQueue.enqueue(element: 1)
cusTomQueue.enqueue(element: 2)
cusTomQueue.enqueue(element: 3)
print(cusTomQueue)
```

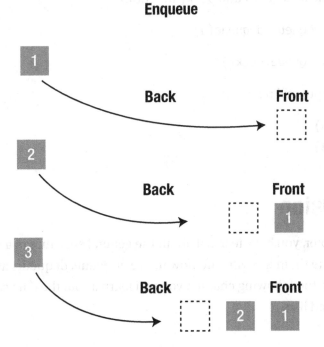

*Figure 5-3.*  *Using the queue methods*

The output will be

**Queue<Int>(data: [1, 2, 3])**

To print out a proper output, the **CustomStringConvertible** extension needs to be added.

```
extension Queue: CustomStringConvertible {
    public var description: String {
        return data.description
    }
}
```

In this case, the output will be

[1, 2, 3]

Using the dequeue() and peek( functions

```
print(cusTomQueue.dequeue())
```

```
print(cusTomQueue.peek())
```

The output will be

**Optional(1)**
**Optional(2)**

# Conclusion

In this chapter, you have learned about the general structure of a queue, how to create them in Swift, and how to use enqueue, dequeue, and peek methods. In the following chapter, you will learn about the data structure type of linked lists.

# CHAPTER 6

# Linked Lists

A linked list is a data structure that holds a group of data items which
represents a sequence. Here each data item is referred to as a node.
The nodes contain data and are interconnected to the next node in the
sequence via their links. More complex forms of the list add additional
links. The main advantage of a linked list is quick insertion and deletion.
The linked list is a linear data structure like arrays, but unlike arrays,
elements are not stored in a contiguous location. Like arrays, a linked list is
a linear data structure (Figure 6-1).

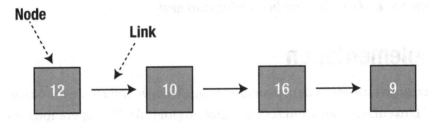

***Figure 6-1.*** *Linear data structure*

There are two main types of linked lists: *singly linked lists* (Figure 6-2),
where each node has only reference to the next node, and *doubly linked
lists* (Figure 6-3), where each node has reference to the previous and next
nodes.

© Elshad Karimov 2020
E. Karimov, *Data Structures and Algorithms in Swift*,
https://doi.org/10.1007/978-1-4842-5769-2_6

***Figure 6-2.*** *Singly linked lists*

***Figure 6-3.*** *Doubly linked lists*

The beginning and end of a list can be tracked using pointers called **head** and **tail** (Figure 6-4).

***Figure 6-4.*** *Tracking the beginning and end*

# Implementation

To create a LinkedList data structure using Swift, we will create the Node and LinkedList classes and several functions for linked list operations. As Swift treats the structures as value type, capturing self for values types is a dangerous practice and discouraged. When we make LinkedList, we use classes because they are the reference type in Swift. Therefore, I would suggest you to create Node as class and make use of the various access specifiers in Swift to achieve the abstraction you are trying to.

# Node

As previously mentioned, a linked list is composed of nodes, so firstly, we need to create a node class using Swift playground. Here again we will use Swift Generics for flexibility.

```
public class Node<nodeType> {
    public var value : nodeType
    public var next : Node?

    public init(value: nodeType) {
        self.value = value
    }
}
extension Node: CustomStringConvertible {
    public var description: String {
        guard let next = next else {
            return "\(value)"
        }
        return "\(value) -> " + String(describing: next) + " " }
}
```

Each node has a value associated with it and a pointer to the next node; that is why we previously declared two variables, and this **Node** is for **SinglyLinkedList**.

# Singly Linked List

Now we have everything we need for Node. To create and modify our LinkedList and to keep track of the list beginnings and ends, we will add a new **LinkedList** class. Firstly, the **SinglyLinkedList** class will be created and then we will continue with **DoublyLinkedList** class later in the chapter.

43

```swift
public class SinglyLinkedList<listType> {

    public var head: Node<listType>?
    public var tail: Node<listType>?

    public var isEmpty: Bool {
        return head == nil
    }

}
extension SinglyLinkedList: CustomStringConvertible {
    public var description: String {
        guard let head = head else {
            return "Empty list"
        }
        return String(describing: head)
    }
}
```

isEmpty is a property that checks if the LinkedList is empty or not.

# Adding New Values to a Linked List

It is possible to add new values to the list by using two methods which are differentiated in terms of performance.

append – New value is added at the end of the list

insert(value:, index:) – To insert an element at a position we need to

# Append

This function adds a new Node to the end of the list. Let us add the following code inside the **SinglyLinkedList** class:

```
public func append(value: listType) {
    let newNode = Node(value: value)
    if var h = head {
        while h.next != nil {
            h = h.next!
        }
        h.next = newNode
    } else {
        head = newNode
    }
}
```

What we are doing here is creating a temporary reference of the header and checking the next reference of the header, and when it is nil, we are at the end of the LinkedList; then we set the next of the last Node to the newNode.

For example: If we create a new LinkedList and append it with new elements, we will see that each time we append the list, a new element is inserted at the end of the list.

```
var newList = SinglyLinkedList<Int>()
newList.append(value: 2)
newList.append(value: 4)
newList.append(value: 6)
newList.append(value: 8)
print(newList)
```

The output will be

```
2 -> 4 -> 6 -> 8
```

# Insert

This function inserts an element at the mentioned index. Let's add the following code inside the **SinglyLinkedList** class.

```
func insert(value : listType, index : Int) {
    let newNode = Node(value: value)

    if (index == 0) {
        newNode.next = head
        head = newNode
    } else {
        var prev = head
        var cur = head
        for _ in 0..<index {
            prev = cur
            cur = cur?.next
        }
        newNode.next = prev?.next
        prev?.next = newNode
    }
}
```

The function first checks if the index is 0 and it adds at the beginning of the list by assigning newNode to the head of the list. Then it finds the previous and current nodes of the mentioned index inside the loop and assign the newNode to the mentioned place.

For example: We will use the previously created and appended list (**2 -> 4 -> 6 -> 8**) to insert odd values in ascending order.

```
print("newList: \(newList)")

newList.insert(value: 1, index: 0)
print("1 has been added to index 0: \(newList)")

newList.insert(value: 3, index: 2)
print("3 has been added to index 2: \(newList)")

newList.insert(value: 5, index: 4)
print("5 has been added to index 4: \(newList)")
```

The output will be

**newList: 2 -> 4 -> 6 -> 8**

**1 has been added to index 0: 1 -> 2 -> 4 -> 6 -> 8**

**3 has been added to index 2: 1 -> 2 -> 3 -> 4 -> 6 -> 8**

**5 has been added to index 4: 1 -> 2 -> 3 -> 4 -> 5 -> 6 -> 8**

# Removing New Values from a Linked List

There are two main methods for removing the nodes from a linked list:

1. `removeLast` – Removes the value at the end of the list

2. `remove(at:)` – Removes a value anywhere in the list

# removeLast

As previously mentioned, it removes the element which is located at the end of the LinkedList, and although we have access to the tail node, without having reference to the previous node, we cannot delete it. Let's add the following code to our LinkedList class:

```
public func removeLast() -> listType? {
    if let h = head {
        if h.next == nil {
            defer {
                head = nil
                tail = nil
            }
            return h.value
        }

        var prev = h
        var curr = h
        while let next = curr.next {
            prev = curr
            curr = next
        }
        prev.next = nil
        tail = prev
        return curr.value

    } else {
        return nil
    }
}
```

First, we check if the head is nil; when it is, we **return** nil – that is what the first **if** statement does. Then, the next **if** checks if the list consists of one node; we remove that node inside **defer** {}. We continue to search for the next node until curr.next **is** nil to find the last node in the list; since the current node is the last one, so by setting prev.next to nil, we disconnect the last node from the list.

## remove(at:)

This function removes an element from the mentioned index.

```
func remove(at position: Int) {
    if head == nil {
        return
    }
    var h = head
    if (position == 0) {
        head = h?.next
        return
    }
    for _ in 0..<position-1 where h != nil {
        h = h?.next
    }
    if h == nil || h?.next == nil {
        return
    }
    let nextToNextNode = h?.next?.next
    h?.next = nextToNextNode
}
```

First, we check if the head is nil, then there is nothing to remove. Then we create an instance of the head, and if the position is 0, we remove the head and set the next value to the head and return; otherwise we loop from 0 to position by assigning head.

Let us see this with an example:

```
print("Initial list: \(newList)")
newList.remove(at: 2)
print("Index 2 is removed: \(newList)")
newList.remove(at: 0)
print("Index 0 is removed: \(newList)")
```

The output will be

```
Initial list: 1 -> 2 -> 3 -> 4 -> 5 -> 6 -> 8
Index 2 is removed: 1 -> 2 -> 4 -> 5 -> 6 -> 8
Index 0 is removed: 2 -> 4 -> 5 -> 6 -> 8
```

# Doubly Linked List

As previously mentioned, a doubly linked list is the list in which each node has reference to the previous and the next nodes. Let's see how this is working by creating a **DoublyLinkedList** class. First, we will create **Node** for doubly list.

```
public class DoubleNode<nodeType> {
    var value: nodeType
    var next: DoubleNode<nodeType>?
    weak var previous: DoubleNode<nodeType>?

    init(value: nodeType) {
        self.value = value
    }
}
```

```swift
extension DoubleNode: CustomStringConvertible {
    public var description: String {
        guard let next = next else {
            return "\(value)"
        }
        return "\(value) -> " + String(describing: next) + " " }
}
```

Each node has a value associated with it, a pointer to the next node, and a pointer to the previous node, and to prevent memory cycles, we declared the previous pointer as weak reference.

After creating the DoubleNode class, it is the right time to continue to create a **DoublyLinkedList** class. We have declared the nodeAt function as a helper function to get an element for a given index.

```swift
public class DoublyLinkedList<listType> {
    var head: DoubleNode<listType>?
    private var tail: DoubleNode<listType>?

    public var isEmpty: Bool {
        return head == nil
    }

public func nodeAt(index: Int) -> DoubleNode<listType>? {
    if index >= 0 {
        var node = head
        var i = index
        while node != nil {
            if i == 0 { return node }
            i -= 1
            node = node!.next
        }
    }
}
```

```
        return nil
    }
}
```

# Append

To add an element to a doubly linked list, the following function is used:

```
func insert(node: DoubleNode<listType>, at index: Int) {
    if index == 0,
        tail == nil {
        head = node
        tail = node
    } else {
        guard let nodeAtIndex = nodeAt(index: index) else {
            print("Index out of bounds.")
            return
        }

        if nodeAtIndex.previous == nil {
            head = node
        }

        node.previous = nodeAtIndex.previous
        nodeAtIndex.previous?.next = node

        node.next = nodeAtIndex
        nodeAtIndex.previous = node
    }
}
```

# Remove Node Method

```
public func remove(node: DoubleNode<listType>) -> listType {
    let previousNode = node.previous
    let nextNode = node.next

    if let prev = previousNode {
      prev.next = nextNode
    } else {
      head = nextNode
    }
    nextNode?.previous = previousNode

    if nextNode == nil {
      tail = previousNode
    }

    node.previous = nil
    node.next = nil

    return node.value
  }
```

# Remove(at:)

```
func remove(at index: Int) {
        var toDeleteNode = nodeAt(index: index)
        guard toDeleteNode != nil else {
            print("Index out of bounds.")
            return
        }

        let previousNode = toDeleteNode?.previous
        let nextNode = toDeleteNode?.next
```

```
    if previousNode == nil {
        head = nextNode
    }

    if toDeleteNode?.next == nil {
        tail = previousNode
    }

    previousNode?.next = nextNode
    nextNode?.previous = previousNode

    toDeleteNode = nil
}
```

# Summary

In this chapter, you have learned about the general structure of linked lists, how to create the singly and doubly linked lists in Swift, and how to use remove, insert, and append methods. In the following chapter, you will learn about the data structure type of hash table.

# CHAPTER 7

# Hash Table

A *hash table* is a data structure of "associative arrays" that groups values
in an index and sorts and retrieves data using a key/value mapping.
It accomplishes the same goal in some cases like Swift dictionaries.
However, the efficiency of hash tables is better than dictionaries. The time
complexity for searching, inserting, and deleting is on average O(1), which
means that regardless of the size of the input operation time remains
constant. This solves the problem of the linear search operation which is
costly and the time complexity is O(n). By calculating the hash value, we
can find the index and place the value in this index and retrieve the value
based on it.

A hash table consists of two parts: index and value. The index is a
computed sequence of numbers or characters which is different from
dictionaries. The process of creating a unique hash is called a hash
algorithm or hash function.

Figure 7-1 illustrates that the input of the city of London always
produces the hash result of 3. The values are stored in buckets and their
position is computed by the hash function. It is a function that can be used
to map a dataset of arbitrary size to a dataset of fixed size, which falls into
the hash table.

© Elshad Karimov 2020
E. Karimov, *Data Structures and Algorithms in Swift*,
https://doi.org/10.1007/978-1-4842-5769-2_7

**Figure 7-1.** *Hash algorithm*

Due to the fact that the time complexity is O(1) for sorting and retrieving, it is ideal for databases where you have a growing set of data.

It is not recommended to use a hash table where you have to iterate over a large amount of data.

# Creating Hash Table

First, a hash element will be created using a class with generic parameters, K (keys) and V (values). Due to the fact that the keys must be Hashable, we need to make sure that K conforms to the Hashable protocol.

```
class HashElement<K: Hashable, V> {
    var key: K
    var value: V?

    init(key: K, value: V?) {
        self.key = key
        self.value = value
    }
}
```

Then, we will define a bucket structure for using our table. As previously mentioned, buckets are a group of values, and as elements will be stored in a noncontiguous fashion, we must define the size for our collection. We use type aliases to provide new names for our hash element which makes our code more readable and clearer. Thus, in Swift it will be as shown here:

```swift
class HashTable<K: Hashable, V> {
    typealias Bucket = [HashElement<K, V>]
    var buckets: [Bucket]

    init(capacity: Int) {
        assert(capacity > 0)
        buckets = Array<Bucket>(repeatElement([], count:
        capacity))
    }
}
```

Finally, we need to create a function that will calculate our index. By using unicodeScalars, a consistent value can be obtained to compute with the hash function, then we take the mode of this value based on bucket count.

```swift
func index(for key: K) -> Int {
    var divisor: Int = 0
    for key in String(describing: key).unicodeScalars {
        divisor += abs(Int(key.value.hashValue))
    }
    return abs(divisor) % buckets.count
}
```

# Retrieving Data from a Hash Table

To retrieve the values using the given key, we will create a method that returns an optional value. This is because if there is no value for our key, it will return nil.

```
func retrieveValue(for key: K) -> V? {
        let index = self.index(for: key)
        for element in buckets[index] {
            if element.key == key {
                return element.value
            }
        }
        return nil
    }
```

The first thing that we need to do here is to find an index of the element based on the given key using index function. Then we iterate through the bucket array to find the relevant element's value and return it; otherwise we return nil.

# Updating a Value in a Hash Table

To update a value in a hash table, we need to create a mutating function to be able to update the properties of a hash table structure. In Swift structures are value types, and the properties of value types cannot be modified; to modify them, we have to use the **mutating** keyword in the instance method. Then we calculate the index and iterate through the buckets array with the enumerated() method and update the value with new one and return oldValue. Using the enumerated() method is very helpful in this case because it iterates over each of the elements while also telling the elements' positions in the array. If the element does not exist in the array, we add it to the array by appending it and returning nil.

```
mutating func updateValue(_ value: V, forKey key: K) -> V? {
        var itemIndex: Int
        itemIndex = self.index(for: key)
```

```
    for (i, element) in buckets[itemIndex].enumerated() {
        if element.key == key {
            let oldValue = element.value
            buckets[itemIndex][i].value = value
            return oldValue
        }
    }
    buckets[itemIndex].append(HashElement(key: key,
    value: value))
    return nil
}
```

# Removing a Value from a Hash Table

Here again we create a mutating function, and based on the calculated index, we iterate over buckets array and find the values using the if condition and remove it based on the index that we get from the enumerated() method.

```
mutating func removeValue(for key: K) -> V? {
    let index = self.index(for: key)
    for (i, element) in buckets[index].enumerated() {
        if element.key == key {
            buckets[index].remove(at: i)
            return element.value
        }
    }
    return nil
}
```

# Summary

In this chapter, you have learned about the general structure of hash table, how to create them in Swift, and how to use retrieve, update, and delete elements from the hash table. In the following chapter, you will learn about the data structure type of tree.

# CHAPTER 8

# Trees

A tree is a nonlinear data structure with hierarchical relationships between its elements; it is basically reversed from a real-life tree. There are many types of trees, and they come in various shapes and sizes. In this chapter, you will learn the basics of using and implementing a tree. A tree consists of nodes and the topmost node is called the root. Each node holds the data and also reference to its child nodes, and if a node does not have a child node, it is called a leaf. Figure 8-1 shows a three-level diagram of a tree. The root is level 0, and as you move down the depth of the tree, the level increases by 1.

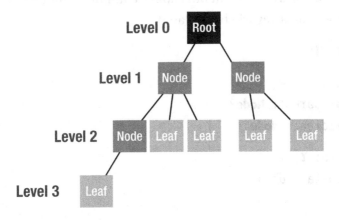

***Figure 8-1.*** *Three levels of a tree*

The total number of children in a node is called degree. The nodes that have the same parent are siblings and they are connected with an edge.

© Elshad Karimov 2020
E. Karimov, *Data Structures and Algorithms in Swift*,
https://doi.org/10.1007/978-1-4842-5769-2_8

The main applications of the trees include

- Manipulate hierarchical data

- Make information easy to search

- Manipulate sorted lists of data

- As a workflow for compositing digital images for visual effects

- Router algorithms

- Form of a multistage decision-making

# Creation

As previously mentioned, a tree is made up of nodes and a node has a value associated with it. Additionally, each node needs to have a list of children and it is handy for each node to have a link to its parent node as well. Each node has one parent but can have multiple children; that is why for child nodes an array will be declared.

```
class Node<T> {

  var data: T
  weak var parent: Node?
  var children: [Node] = []

  init(data: T) {
    self.data = data
  }
}
```

So what we have done here is to set the data of the node in the init() method, and as a node can have multiple children, children array is declared which is made up of nodes. We have set the reference of parent node to weak var to prevent strong cycles which can cause memory leaks.

Finally, as our tree type is a generic type, we need a method for printing the tree. By adding the following code inside the Node class, we can define the printing method:

```
func printNodeData() -> [String] {
        return ["\(self.data)"] + self.children.flatMap{$0.
        printNodeData()}.map{"    "+$0}
   }
func printTree() {
        let text = printNodeData().joined(separator: "\n")
        print(text)
   }
```

We convert the data to a string by enclosing it in "\()" and we use standard flatMap and map methods to print the node data properly.

## Insertion

We will declare the add(child:) method to handle insertion to our tree.

```
func add(child: Node) {
     children.append(child)
     child.parent = self
   }
```

We append the children array which is made up of nodes, and set child parent. To understand how this addition method works, let us write the following code in the playground outside our class:

```
let drinks = Node(data: "Drinks")
let type1 = Node<String>(data: "Cold")
let type2 = Node<String>(data: "Hot")

drinks.add(child: type1)
drinks.add(child: type2)
```

```
type2.add(child: Node(data: "Latte"))
type1.add(child: Node(data: "Cola"))
type1.add(child: Node(data: "Fanta"))
drinks.printTree()
```

The output will be

```
Drink
    Cold
        Cola
        Fanta
    Hot
        Latte
```

Hierarchical structures are natural candidates for tree structures, so here we have defined six different nodes and organized them in a logical hierarchy. This arrangement corresponds to the structure shown in Figure 8-2.

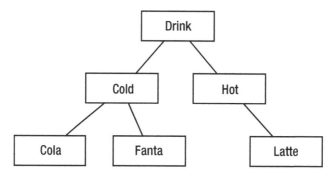

***Figure 8-2.*** *Sample tree*

# Searching Data

Add the following method inside the Node class for the search algorithm of the tree data structure that we declared. This method searches for a value in the tree, and if the data exist in the tree, it returns the node associated with the value; otherwise the return is nil. If the data is found in the current node, we return self which is the current node. The next line of the code loops through the children array and every time we call each child's search method which will recursively iterate through all the children, and if any of the nodes have a match, it will return the node. Finally, we return nil if no data is matched.

```
func search(element: T) -> Node? {
    if element == self.data {
      return self
    }
    for child in children {
      if let result = child.search(element: element) {
        return result
      }
    }
    return nil
  }
```

Let's try this using the playground outside our class.

```
let latte = drinks.search(element: "Latte")

if let result = latte {
    result.printTree()
}
```

The output will be

**Latte**

As previously mentioned, when you do a search inside a tree, an iteration through children will be done. This iteration is different from the normal ones, which is a bit complicated.

There are different types of tree data structure and some of them will be discussed in the next chapters.

- Trie

- Binary tree

- Red–black tree

- R tree

# Conclusion

In this chapter, you have learned about the general structure of a tree, how to implement it in Swift, and how to declare, search, and add methods for it. In the following chapters, you will learn more about the different types of tree data structure.

# CHAPTER 9

# Trie Data Structure

In this chapter, we will review Trie (pronounced as try) data structures and how to implement it using Swift. A Trie is a tree-based data structure that organizes information in a hierarchy. While most of the other structures are designed to manipulate generic data, Trie is often used with Strings – it is used for storing words in a way which enables fast lookups. Since Trie stores characters at each node, it is very efficient for prefix matching in the English language.

## Why a Trie?

A Trie is very useful for storing the English language, and it has the following advantages which might be a perfect substitute for a hash table data structure:

- – Better worst-case time complexity.

- – No key collisions.

- – No hashing algorithm.

- – It is alphabetically ordered.

Additionally, if we use an array for dealing more than a thousand words, the complexity of searching for a particular word is O(k∗n), where k is the longest string and n is the number of words that needs to be checked. The trie structure solves this problem; as each node can represent a single character, it creates a word by tracing the collection of characters from a root to a node.

© Elshad Karimov 2020
E. Karimov, *Data Structures and Algorithms in Swift*,
https://doi.org/10.1007/978-1-4842-5769-2_9

# How It Works

As previously mentioned, a trie organizes the data in a hierarchy and the last node in each string is marked as a finalNode. Let's build a sample dictionary to see how a trie works. Suppose we have four words: apple, apex, code, and comb. So our corresponding trie structure looks like Figure 9-1.

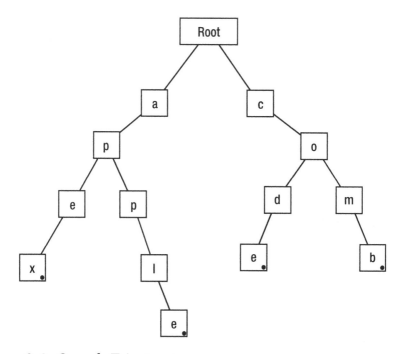

***Figure 9-1.*** *Sample Trie structure*

As you can see, multiple words can share the same letters, and the way that the trie structure organizes them improves the performance of this structure. To illustrate the performance advantages of the trie, consider the following example where we need to find the words with prefix CO. It is obvious that first we need to go to the node containing C and this excludes other branches of the trie from the search operation which makes our search faster. Then, we will find the words that have the next letter O and shift to this node and again exclude the others. Since this is the end of our prefix, the trie will return all branches of the O node. In our case, it will be code and comb. Suppose we have thousands of words in our trie, so the number of branches that we exclude is substantial and this makes less comparison and leads to faster search.

# Implementation

The first thing we need to do is to create a TrieNode, as we did for the previous data structure. So open Xcode and create a new playground file called Trie.swift and insert the following code:

```swift
public class TrieNode<K: Hashable> {
  var value: K?
  weak var parent: TrieNode?
  var children: [K: TrieNode] = [:]
  var isFinal = false

  init(value: K? = nil, parent: TrieNode? = nil) {
    self.value = value
    self.parent = parent
  }
}
```

First we create a value variable which is of type K that holds the data for the node. Due to the fact that the root of the trie does not have a key, we declare this variable as optional. Then, the parent node is declared with a weak reference to TrieNode; this is because of the remove method that we will create later. In the third line, we create children as a dictionary, because a node in a trie holds multiple branches. isFinal is an indicator for the end of a String.

The next thing that we will do is to create a Trie itself. So let's create a new class as shown in the following code:

```
public class Trie {
    private let rootNode: TrieNode<Character>

    init() {
        rootNode = TrieNode<Character>()
    }
}
```

Here we declare a rootNode for our **Trie** using the **Character** type, because we are implementing a **Trie** for the English language, and inside init method, an empty **TrieNode** is initialized.

## Insert

A Trie is efficient for inserting values because it always reuses the existing nodes. For example, code and comb are using the same nodes of C and O. To insert a new node into our Trie, create the following insert method inside the Trie class:

```
func insert(word: String) {
        guard !word.isEmpty else { return }
        var curNode = rootNode
        let characters = Array(word.lowercased())
        var curIndex = 0
        while curIndex < characters.count {
            let character = characters[curIndex]
            if let child = curNode.children[character] {
                curNode = child
```

```
    } else {
        curNode.children[character] = TrieNode(value:
        character, parent: curNode)
        curNode = curNode.children[character]!
    }

    curIndex += 1

    if curIndex == characters.count {
        curNode.isFinal = true
    }
   }
 }
```

Here, first we check if the string is empty, and if it is, there is nothing to insert. Then we create a reference to rootNode which will be used to create new nodes. Since each node contains one letter, we create an array of characters from the string that is passed as a parameter. We use curIndex variable to keep track of the iteration through a characters array. As it reaches the count of the characters array, the iteration stops. Inside the if condition, we check if the character that we are trying to insert exists within the children; if so, we move the curNode reference to the next node and there is no need for insertion. Otherwise, we add a character into the current children dictionary and the mode of the curNode reference to the new node.

It is obvious that we need to indicate the end of the word as well and isFinal property of the node is responsible for this.

# Query

This function is responsible to check if a given word exists in the Trie, and if so, it returns true; otherwise the return value will be false. It is very similar to the **Insert** method, but here instead of creating a node, we only check its existence and isFinal value must be set to true in order to return true. Let's write the following code inside the **Trie** class and see how it works:

```
func query(word: String) -> Bool {
        let characters = Array(word.lowercased())
        var node : TrieNode? = rootNode
        for character in characters {
          node = node?.children[character]
          if node == nil {
            return false
          }
        }
        return node!.isFinal
  }
```

Here again, we create a characters array from the given word and iterate through it; if the node is nil, it means the searched character does not exist, so we return false; otherwise we will reach the end of the **String** and return isFinal value which is true.

## Remove

This method is similar to the query method, but we change the isFinal value to false which removes the termination for the word, and as there is no termination, this word cannot be accounted as a word in the Trie. Let's write this code inside the **Trie** class:

```
func remove(word: String) {
        let characters = Array(word.lowercased())
        var node : TrieNode? = rootNode
        for character in characters {
          node = node?.children[character]
```

```
    if node == nil {
        return
    }
  }
  node!.isFinal = false
}
```

In Figure 9-2 you will notice that even though we delete the code string from the Trie, it still appears, but only missing termination.

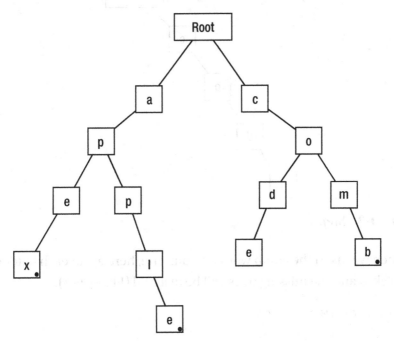

***Figure 9-2.*** *A Trie after removing of an element*

Let's check our three methods in a sample. First we create a Trie using our Trie class, and by using the previously declared method, we insert, query, and remove values from it.

The first step is to declare a Trie data structure, and by using the insert method, we insert nodes.

```
var myTrie = Trie()
myTrie.insert(word: "code")
```

Here, the insertion checks whether the letters of the "code" exist in the node; if not, it creates new nodes for each of them (Figure 9-3).

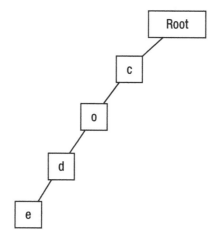

***Figure 9-3.*** *Step 1*

Then we insert the comb word into our Trie; here again each letter will be checked and the missing ones will be inserted (Figure 9-4).

```
myTrie.insert(word: "comb")
```

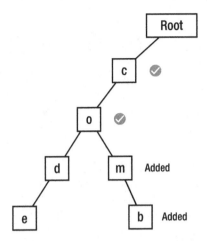

***Figure 9-4.*** *Adding comb*

Then by using the query method, we can check whether the inserted words exist in the data structure or not.

```
print(myTrie.query(word: "code"))
myTrie.remove(word: "code")
print(myTrie.query(word: "code"))
```

The output will be

**true**
**false**

This means that when we query the code first, it exists in the **Trie**, but the second time, it is missing because we used the remove method to remove it.

# Conclusion

In this chapter, you have learned about the Trie data structure, which provides great performance in regard to prefix matching. You also mastered how to insert, remove, and query inside the Trie structure.

# CHAPTER 10

# Binary Tree

In the previous chapter, you have learned about the basic tree structure where each node can have unlimited children. Binary trees are tree data structures in which each node has at most two children, often referred to as the left and right children. In this chapter, you will learn the main properties of binary data structure and how to implement it.

## Binary Tree Primer

The basic structure of a binary tree is shown in Figure 10-1.

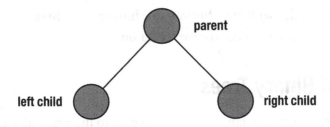

***Figure 10-1.*** *Basic binary tree*

Before continuing to the properties and the types of binary tree, let's identify some terms related to it.

> Node depth – The number of edges from the node to the root node. A root depth is 0.

Node height – The number of edges on the longest oath from the node to a leaf. Leaf height is 0.

Tree height – From the root node to the farthest leaf.

# Properties of Binary Tree

1.  The maximum number of nodes at level "**i**" of the binary tree is $2^{i-1}$.

    The level in the root is $1 \rightarrow 2^{1-1}=1$. Due to the fact that every node has at most two children, the next level has twice the nodes, $2*2^{i-1}$.

2.  If the height of the binary tree is "h", the maximum number of nodes is $2^h-1$. The height of a tree is the maximum number of nodes on the root to the leaf path.

3.  The number of leaf nodes is always one more than the nodes with two children in a binary tree where every node has zero or two children.

# Types of Binary Trees

Binary trees are a simple concept; they are easy to understand, easy to implement, and work well and fast. There are several different types of binary trees:

1.  Full binary tree (Figure 10-2) – Each node has zero or two children, but not one.

## Full Binary Tree

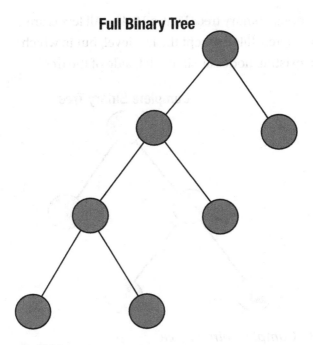

*Figure 10-2.*  *Full binary tree*

2. Perfect binary tree (Figure 10-3) – All nodes have two children and the same depth.

## Perfect Binary Tree

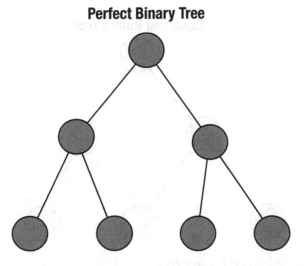

*Figure 10-3.*  *Perfect binary tree*

3.  Complete binary tree (Figure 10-4) – All levels are completely filled except the last level, but in which the existing nodes are in the left side of the tree.

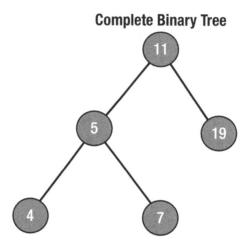

***Figure 10-4.*** *Complete binary tree*

4.  Balanced binary tree (Figure 10-5) – Each leaf is "not more than a certain distance" from the root node than any other leaf.

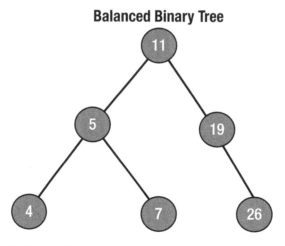

***Figure 10-5.*** *Balanced binary tree*

# Implementation

To implement the binary tree data structure, we need a node that must have at least the following elements:

- Key/value for data container

- References to the left and right children nodes

- Reference to a parent node

So let's define a class called BTNode and add the following code in it:

```
class BTNode<T> {
    var value: T
    var leftChild: BTNode<T>?
    var rightChild: BTNode<T>?

    init(_ value: T,_ leftChild: BTNode?,_ rightChild: BTNode?) {
        self.value = value
        self.rightChild = rightChild
        self.leftChild = leftChild
    }
}
```

Here we have made our class generic in order to allow any kind of value type inside the value property. Our binary tree node has a property called value to store key data. Additionally, it has two variables to store the left and right children, and these are the minimum required properties that we need to define the binary tree node.

# Tree Traversal (Also Known As Tree Search)

Tree traversals refer to the process of checking or updating each node in a tree data structure once. They are classified by the visiting order of nodes. Unlike linear data structures which can only be traversed in a linear order, the tree data structures can be traversed in various ways. There are three common ways to traverse them:

- In-order

- Pre-order

- Post-order

# In-Order Traversal

In-order traversal (Figure 10-6) first visits the left child value, then the current node value and finally the right child value. If our binary tree is ordered, in-order traversal visits the nodes in ascending order.

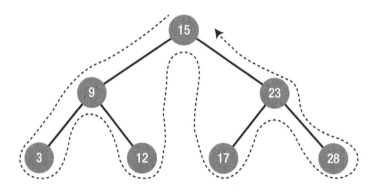

**In - order : 3, 9, 12, 15, 17, 23, 28**

*Figure 10-6.* *In-order traversal*

It can be clearly seen that it prints the nodes in ascending order.

The following function shows how to implement the in-order traversal in Swift, so copy the following code to the BTNode class:

```
func inorderTraversal(_ btNode: BTNode<T>?) {
    guard let _ = btNode else { return }
    self.inorderTraversal(btNode?.leftChild)
```

```
    print("\(btNode!.value)", terminator: "  ")
    self.inorderTraversal(btNode?.rightChild)
}
```

Firstly, we check if the current node is empty or nil, then we traverse the subtree by recursively calling the in-order function and display the data. When the left subtree traversal is finished, we traverse the right subtree by calling recursively the in-order function.

Let's see in the preceding example how it works. First, we create the tree node as previously shown and call the inorderTraversal function based on the root parameter.

```
let node3 = BTNode(3,nil,nil)
let node12 = BTNode(12,nil,nil)
let node17 = BTNode(17,nil,nil)
let node28 = BTNode(28,nil,nil)
let node9 = BTNode(9,node3,node12)
let node23 = BTNode(23,node17,node28)
let root = BTNode(15,node9,node23)

let t = BTNode(0,nil,nil)
t.inorderTraversal(root)
```

The output will be

**3   9   12   15   17   23   28**

# Pre-Order Traversal

Pre-order traversal (Figure 10-7) always starts from the current node, then continue to visit the left and right children.

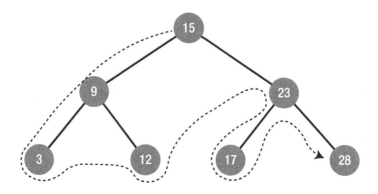

**Pre - order : 15, 9, 3, 12, 23, 17, 28**

***Figure 10-7.*** *Pre-order traversal*

Let's create the pre-order traversal function. Copy the following code into the BTNode class after the inorderTraversal function. First, traversal visits the current node and then recursively visits the left and right nodes.

```
func preorderTraversal(_ btNode: BTNode<T>?) {
    guard let _ = btNode else { return }
    print("\(btNode!.value)", terminator: "  ")
    self.preorderTraversal(btNode?.leftChild)
    self.preorderTraversal(btNode?.rightChild)
}
```

Let's run this function for the previously created tree.

```
let t = BTNode(0,nil,nil)
t.preorderTraversal(root)
```

The output will be

**15   9   3   12   23   17   28**

# Post-Order Traversal

Post-order traversal (Figure 10-8) first visits the leftmost node, then the right node and then its parent. After that it visits the previous parent with the same rule.

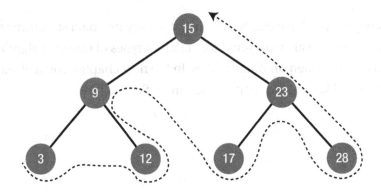

**Post - order : 3, 12, 9, 17, 28, 23, 15**

***Figure 10-8.*** *Post-order traversal*

Let's create the post-order function inside the BTNode class. Copy the following code inside the mentioned class and we will run it for the same tree structure that we have created:

```
func postorderTraversal(_ btNode: BTNode<T>?) {
        guard let _ = btNode else { return }
        self.postorderTraversal(btNode?.leftChild)
        self.postorderTraversal(btNode?.rightChild)
        print("\(btNode!.value)", terminator: "  ")
    }
```

Let us run it:

```
let t = BTNode(0,nil,nil)
t.postorderTraversal(root)
```

The output will be

**3   12   9   17   28   23   15**

# Conclusion

In this chapter, you have learned about the binary tree data structure and its different types. You also mastered the different types of traversal algorithms that can be performed on Binary Trees. In the next chapter, you will learn about a special kind of binary tree, the Binary Search Tree.

# CHAPTER 11

# Binary Search Tree

A Binary Search Tree (BST) is a binary tree in which each node has at most two children, and it facilitates fast search, insertion, and deletion operations. The time complexity of each operation is O(log n), which is considerably faster than linear search. The two main characteristics of the Binary Search Trees are as follows:

- The value of the left node must be lesser than the value of its parent.
- The value of the right node must be greater than or equal to the value of its parent.

Figure 11-1 shows the basic structure of the Binary Search Tree.

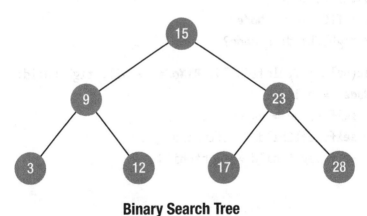

**Binary Search Tree**

***Figure 11-1.*** *Basic structure of the Binary Search Tree*

© Elshad Karimov 2020
E. Karimov, *Data Structures and Algorithms in Swift*,
https://doi.org/10.1007/978-1-4842-5769-2_11

The structure of the Binary Search Tree makes it more efficient for searching operations, because in each step of the search process, the algorithm makes two assumptions:

1. If the searched value is less than the current node, it continues to the left subtree.

2. If it is greater than the current node, it continues to the right subtree.

These two assumptions eliminate unnecessary searches and reduce the search path by half in each step, and this makes it very efficient.

# Implementation

Firstly, we need to create **Node** and **Binary Tree Search** classes, and here we will use the BTNode class that we created in the previous chapter for binary tree.

```
class BTNode<T> {
    var value: T
    var leftChild: BTNode?
    var rightChild: BTNode?

    init(value: T, leftChild: BTNode? = nil, rightChild:
    BTNode? = nil) {
        self.value = value
        self.leftChild = leftChild
        self.rightChild = rightChild
    }
}
```

Based on the declared Tree Node, we will create a Binary Search Tree class.

```
class BinarySearchTree<T: Comparable & CustomStringConvertible>
{

    private var rootNode: BTNode<T>?

}
```

The class conforms with the **Comparable** protocol to guarantee that the type will use the comparison operators, and the **CustomStringConvertible** protocol is used for the description of different data types. Let's continue to add the insert function to this class.

# Insert

Insertion to a BST follows the previously mentioned two assumptions; we only need to find the location for the insertion and it is an O(log n) operation. To illustrate the power of Binary Search Trees, let's compare the insertion performance of arrays against them. Assume we want to insert 0 to an array. To insert a new element to the array, first we secure an additional space at the end of the array, then the data is shifted one element at a time, and then the element can be inserted (Figure 11-2).

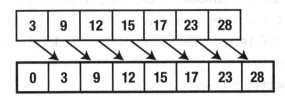

*Figure 11-2.* *Array Insertion*

In this example, an element of zero is inserted in the front of the array, and all elements are shifted by one position which means that the time complexity of insertion to the array is O(n).

Contrary to the arrays, the insertion to Binary Search Trees is faster. Based on the mentioned assumptions, we only need three steps to find a location for an element of zero as shown in Figure 11-3, and the time complexity for this process is O(log n).

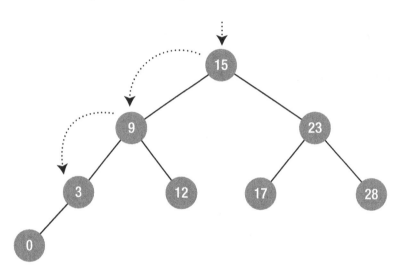

***Figure 11-3.*** *BST insertion sample*

```
func insert(insertedValue : T) {
        let inNode = BTNode(value: insertedValue)
        if let rootNode = self.rootNode {
            self.insertNode(rootNode: rootNode, inNode: inNode)
        } else {
            self.rootNode = inNode
        }
    }
```

```
private func insertNode(rootNode: BTNode<T>, inNode:
BTNode<T>) {
    if rootNode.value > inNode.value {
        if let leftChild = rootNode.leftChild {
            self.insertNode(rootNode: leftChild, inNode:
            inNode)
        } else {
            rootNode.leftChild = inNode
        }
    } else {
        if let rightChild = rootNode.rightChild {
            self.insertNode(rootNode: rightChild, inNode:
            inNode)
        } else {
            rootNode.rightChild = inNode
        }
    }
}
```

To make our code more readable, I have created two separate
functions and called insertNode function inside the insert function; that
is why the insertNode method is private. Inside the insertNode function,
first we compare the rootNode value with the value of the node that will
be inserted. If the rootNode value is greater, we add a new node to the
leftChild node; otherwise we add it to the rightChild node. Inside the insert
function, first we check if the rootNode exists, and if it does, we call the
insertNode method; otherwise we add a new node as rootNode.

# Search

The process of searching is similar to the insertion, which conforms with the two mentioned assumptions. The only difference is that when the node data gets matched with input data, it will return successfully; otherwise invalid message will be returned. To make it clear, let's compare the search in an array within the BST. To find the element 28 in an array, we need to compare the elements within the array one by one until we find it, which is O(n) time complexity (Figure 11-4).

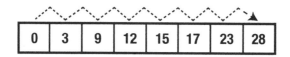

***Figure 11-4.*** *Array search*

On the other hand, this is not the case in the BST. The two main assumptions of the BST allow us to make the search process faster as shown in Figure 11-5.

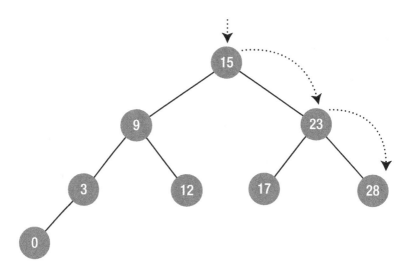

***Figure 11-5.*** *BST search sample*

For each step in the BST, the search algorithm makes two assumptions – if the value is less than the current node, it continues to the left subtree; otherwise, it continues to the right subtree. This helps to avoid unnecessary checks and makes the time complexity O(log n).

```
func searchValue(sValue: T) {
        self.searchNode(rootNode: self.rootNode, searchValue:
        sValue)
    }

    private func searchNode(rootNode: BTNode<T>?,
    searchValue: T) {
        guard let rootNode = rootNode else {
            print("The node of \(searchValue) does not exist")
            return
        }
        print("Root Node \(rootNode.value)")
        if searchValue > rootNode.value {
            self.searchNode(rootNode: rootNode.rightChild,
            searchValue: searchValue)
        } else if searchValue < rootNode.value {
            self.searchNode(rootNode: rootNode.leftChild,
            searchValue: searchValue)
        } else {
            print("Node found: \(rootNode.value)")
        }
    }
```

# Example

Let's use insert and search functions in real example and see how they work. We will call insert function inside the iteration to insert values from 0 to 5, and then using the search function, we will search for number 4.

```
var binaryST = BinarySearchTree<Int>()
for i in 0..<5 {
    binaryST.insert(insertedValue: i) }
binaryST.searchValue(sValue: 4)
```

The output will be

**Root Node 0**
**Root Node 1**
**Root Node 2**
**Root Node 3**
**Root Node 4**
**Node found: 4**

# Delete

There are some cases that need to be taken into account when deleting an element from a Binary Search Tree.

## Deleting a Leaf

To delete a leaf from a Binary Search Tree, no extra action is needed; we just remove the leaf node from the tree (Figure 11-6).

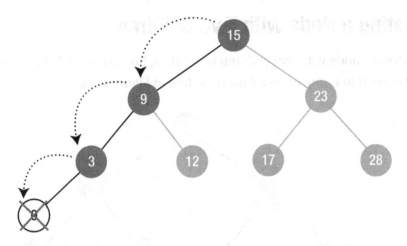

***Figure 11-6.*** *BST deleting a leaf*

# Deleting a Node with One Child

To delete a node with one child, first a node is deleted and then the child node needs to be reconnected to the rest of the tree (Figure 11-7).

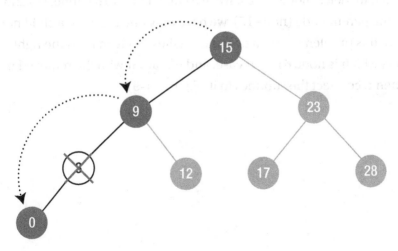

***Figure 11-7.*** *BST deleting a node with a child*

# Deleting a Node with Two Children

Removing a node with two children is not straightforward. Let's imagine that we want to remove node 9 from the tree in Figure 11-8.

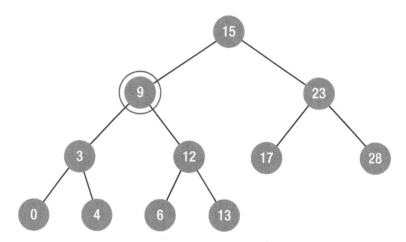

***Figure 11-8.*** *BST deleting a node with two children*

When we delete node 9, we have two child nodes to reconnect (3 and 12), but in the parent node (node 15), we have only one place for a child node. To solve this problem, we will take the smallest node in from the right subtree, which is node 6 in our case, and replace it with the removed node and then reconnect the subtrees to it (Figure 11-9).

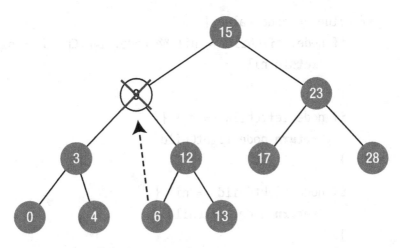

***Figure 11-9.***  *BST deletion sample*

Before creating the remove function, we need to declare the minimum variable in the Binary Tree Node (BTNode) to find the minimum value when removing a node with two children. Add the following code inside the Binary Search Tree class:

```
extension BTNode {
    var min: BTNode {
      return leftChild?.min ?? self
    }
}

func removeValue(sValue: T) {
        rootNode = removeNode(rNode: rootNode, value: sValue)
    }

private func removeNode(rNode: BTNode<T>?, value : T) ->
BTNode<T>? {
        guard let node = rNode else {
            return nil
        }
```

```
        if value == node.value {
            if node.leftChild == nil && node.rightChild == nil {
                return nil
            }

            if node.leftChild == nil {
                return node.rightChild
            }

            if node.rightChild == nil {
                return node.leftChild
            }

            node.value = node.rightChild!.min.value
            node.rightChild = removeNode(rNode: node.
            rightChild, value: node.value)
        } else if value < node.value {
            node.leftChild = removeNode(rNode: node.leftChild,
            value: value)
        } else {
            node.rightChild = removeNode(rNode: node.
            rightChild, value: value)
        }

        return node

    }
```

Inside removeNode, first we check if the node that will be removed exists and then we continue to check the preceding cases. First, the if condition checks if there are no children and, if so, returns nil, which

means that deletes the current node. The if node.leftChild == nil and
if node.rightChild == nil conditions check whether the left or right
children exist and, if yes, reconnect them with the tree, and this is our
case 2. Then we find the minimum value and reconnect it with the tree.

Let's see how this works.

```
var binaryST = BinarySearchTree<Int>()
for i in 0..<5 {
    binaryST.insert(insertedValue: i) }
binaryST.searchValue(sValue: 4)
binaryST.removeValue(sValue: 4)
binaryST.searchValue(sValue: 4)
```

The output will be

**Root Node 0**
**Root Node 1**
**Root Node 2**
**Root Node 3**
**Root Node 4**
**Node found: 4**
**Root Node 0**
**Root Node 1**
**Root Node 2**
**Root Node 3**
**The node of 4 does not exist**

As you can see after calling the remove function for 4, it does not exist
in the tree anymore.

# Conclusion

In this chapter, you have learned about Binary Search Tree and how to implement various methods such as search, insert, and remove. The Binary Search Tree is a very powerful data structure when managing sorted data in terms of performance. In the next chapter, you will learn another type of tree which is red–black tree.

# CHAPTER 12

# Red–Black Tree

A red–black tree (RBT) is a type of Binary Search Tree where a new parameter – color for each node – has been defined (Figure 12-1). We learned that after some insert and delete operations, the Binary Search Trees become unbalanced which creates a linked list. Red–black trees solve this problem by balancing elements. Each node has a color which can be black or red. Thus, when declaring a node for the RBT, it must contain a key/value, a color, the reference to a parent node, and the references for the children nodes. RBTs are very useful for worst-case scenarios when processing search, insertion, and deletion operations.

Properties of RBT

- Each node must have a color: red or black.

- The root node is always black.

- Nil leaves are always black.

- If a node is red node, the children must be black.

- For each node, all simple paths from the node to the descendant leaves contain the same number of black.

© Elshad Karimov 2020
E. Karimov, *Data Structures and Algorithms in Swift*,
https://doi.org/10.1007/978-1-4842-5769-2_12

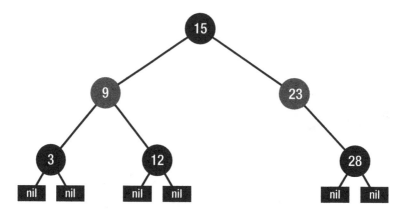

**Figure 12-1.** *Example of a red–black tree*

Figure 12-1 shows the basic structure of red–black trees.

A Red–black tree is a self-balancing tree – the limitations put on the node colors ensure that any simple path from the root to a leaf is not more than twice as long as any other such path. It helps in maintaining the self-balancing property of the red–black tree.

# Implementation

To implement the red–black tree data structure, we need a node that must have at least the following elements:

- Key/value for data container

- References to the left and right children nodes

- Reference to a parent node

- Color variable

So let's define a class called **RBNode** and add the following code in it. We know that the color can be either red or black; that is why before defining a class, let's create enum for color variable which consists of two colors – black and red.

```
private enum RBNodeColor {
  case red
  case black
}
```

And the RBNode class will be

```
public class RBNode<T: Comparable>: Equatable {
        var color: RBNodeColor = .black
    var key: T?
    var leftChild: RBNode<T>?
    var rightChild: RBNode<T>?
    weak var parent: RBNode<T>?

    public init(key: T?, leftChild: RBNode<T>?, rightChild:
    RBNode<T>?, parent: RBNode<T>?) {
        self.key = key
        self.leftChild = leftChild
        self.rightChild = rightChild
        self.parent = parent
        self.leftChild?.parent = self
        self.rightChild?.parent = self
    }
}
//Equatable protocol
extension RBNode {
  static public func == <T>(lhs: RBNode<T>, rhs: RBNode<T>) ->
  Bool {
    return lhs.key == rhs.key
  }
}
```

We created the required variables and initialized them inside init method, and our class must conform to the **Comparable** and **Equatable** protocols. The extension at the end is added for **Equatable** protocol to be conformed.

The next thing that we will do is to create a red–black tree itself. So let's create a new class as shown in the following, but before doing so, we need to add **convenience** initialization inside the **RBNode** class to be able to initialize it with nil values. So add the following methods in **RBNode** class after public **init** method:

```
public convenience init(key: T?) {
    self.init(key: key, leftChild: RBNode(), rightChild:
    RBNode(), parent: RBNode())
}

// For initializing the nullLeaf
public convenience init() {
  self.init(key: nil, leftChild: nil, rightChild: nil,
  parent: nil)
  self.color = .black
}
```

Then our **RedBlackTree** class will be like this:

```
public class RedBlackTree<T: Comparable> {
    public typealias RBTreeNode = RBNode<T>
    private var root: RBTreeNode
    private var size = 0
    let nullLeaf = RBTreeNode()

    public init() {
        root = nullLeaf
    }
}
```

Here we created **typealias** to make our code more readable and declared root and nullLeaf for the tree.

There are various operations that can be performed on a red–black tree. There might be cases that red–black tree properties that are previously mentioned are violated by the operations such as insertion and deletion, so in this case rotation operation is used to maintain the properties.

# Rotation

In a rotation one subtree gets one level closer to the root and another subtree gets further from the root.

There are two types of rotation:

- Left rotation - shown in Figure 12-2

- Right rotation - shown in Figure 12-3

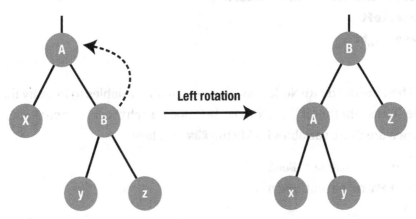

*Figure 12-2.* *Visualization of a left rotation operation*

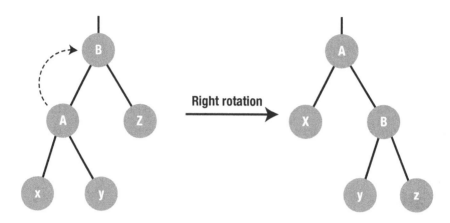

*Figure 12-3.* *Visualization of a right rotation operation*

The following code shows how to implement the rotation method for a red–black tree. First, we need another enum for rotation direction, which might be right or left.

```
private enum RotationDirection {
  case left
  case right
}
```

Then inside the RBNode class, we need a few variables to identify the node status whether it is leafNode, leftNode, rightNode, or rootNode. So let's declare these variables inside the **RBNode** class.

```
var isRootNode: Bool {
  return parent == nil
}

var isLeafNode: Bool {
  return rightChild == nil && leftChild == nil
}
```

```
var isNullLeaf: Bool {
  return key == nil && isLeafNode && color == .black
}

var isLeftNode: Bool {
  return parent?.leftChild === self
}

var isRightNode: Bool {
  return parent?.rightChild === self
}
```

rootNode is a node that does not have a parent value, so that is why isRootNode returns true when the parent is nil.

leafNode is a node that does not have either children – right and left. Here isLeafNode returns true when both children are nil.

nullLeaf is a node where the key is nil and its color is always black. Here isNullLeaf returns true when the key is null and it is leafNode and the color is black.

isLeftNode returns true when a parent node's left child node is identical with the current node. Note that it is not equal, and we use here identical operator (===). This means that they reference the same point in the memory. The same principles are accepted for isRightNode here.

After declaring these variables in the **RBNode** class, we continue to create the rotate method inside the **RedBlackTree** class.

```
private func rotate(node A: RBTreeNode, direction:
RotationDirection) {
        var nodeB: RBTreeNode? = RBNode()

        //Step 1
        switch direction {
        case .left:
          nodeB = A.rightChild
```

```
      A.rightChild = nodeB?.leftChild
      A.rightChild?.parent = A
    case .right:
      nodeB = A.leftChild
      A.leftChild = nodeB?.rightChild
      A.leftChild?.parent = A
    }

    //Step 2
    nodeB?.parent = A.parent
    if A.isRootNode {
      if let node = nodeB {
        root = node
      }
    } else if A.isLeftNode {
      A.parent?.leftChild = nodeB
    } else if A.isRightNode {
      A.parent?.rightChild = nodeB
    }

    //Step 3
    switch direction {
    case .left:
      nodeB?.leftChild = A
    case .right:
      nodeB?.rightChild = A
    }
    A.parent = nodeB
  }
```

For the explanation of this code, let's take as an example the left rotation and visualize it step by step.

We assume that the direction is equal to **.left**.

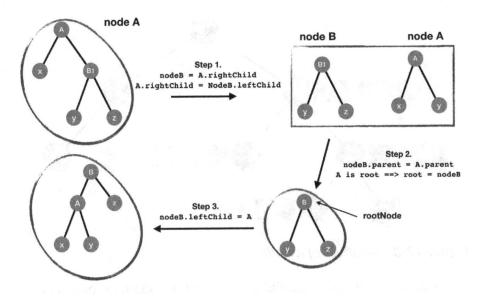

***Figure 12-4.*** *Left rotation steps*

Figure 12-4 illustrates the steps from the rotation method.

## Insertion

The insertion to a red–black tree is performed as a standard insertion to a Binary Search Tree. But the problem is after insertion the tree might not be a valid red–black tree anymore. So to tackle this problem, we create a fixInsert method. Before declaring this method, let's add three variables such as siblingNode, grandparentNode, and uncleNode into the **RBNode** class. In Figure 12-5, these variables are shown visually.

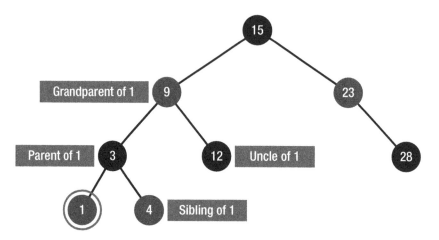

**Figure 12-5.** *Relatives of a node*

As shown in the figure, the sibling of Node 1 is Node 4, the parent of Node 1 is Node 3, the uncle of Node 1 is Node 12, and the grandparent of 1 is Node 9.

Let's copy the following variables inside the RBNode class:

```
var grandparentNode: RBNode? {
    return parent?.parent
}

var siblingNode: RBNode? {
    if isLeftNode {
      return parent?.rightChild
    } else {
      return parent?.leftChild
    }
}

var uncleNode: RBNode? {
    return parent?.siblingNode
}
```

After declaring these variables inside the RBNode class, copy the following code inside the **RedBlackTree** class:

```swift
private func fixInsert(node z: RBTreeNode) {
        if !z.isNullLeaf {
            guard let parentZ = z.parent else {
                return
            }
            //If both Z and its parent are red ↗ violation of
            red-black tree property, so we need to fix it.
            if parentZ.color == .red {
                guard let uncle = z.uncleNode else {
                    return
                }

                //Case 1: Uncle red ↗ recolor and move z.
                if uncle.color == .red {
                    parentZ.color = .black
                    uncle.color = .black
                    if let grandParentZ = parentZ.parent {
                        grandParentZ.color = .red
                        //Move z to the grandparent and check
                        again.
                        fixInsert(node: grandParentZ)
                    }
                }
            } else {
                // Case 2: Uncle black
                var zNew = z
                //Case 2.1: z right node ↗ rotate
                if parentZ.isLeftNode && z.isRightNode {
                    zNew = parentZ
                    rotate(node: zNew, direction: .left)
```

```
            } else if parentZ.isRightNode && z.isLeftNode {
                zNew = parentZ
                rotate(node: zNew, direction: .right)
            }
            //Case 2.2: z is left child ↗ recolor + rotate
            zNew.parent?.color = .black
            if let grandparentZnew = zNew.grandparentNode {
                grandparentZnew.color = .red
                if z.isLeftNode {
                    rotate(node: grandparentZnew,
                    direction: .right)
                } else {
                    rotate(node: grandparentZnew,
                    direction: .left)
                }
            }
        }
    }
    root.color = .black
}
```

It can be seen that there are two cases here and the second case includes two types in itself.

Case 1: z's uncle is red.

1. Change the color of the parent and uncle as black.

2. Change the color of the grandparent as red.

3. Call the fixInsert method for the grandparent of z.

Case 2: z's uncle is black – there can be two cases here.

Case 2.1: z is the right node – here, we move z upward, so z's parent is the newZ and then we rotate around this newZ.

Case 2.1: z is the left child. In this case, we recolor z.parent to black and z.grandparent to red. Then we rotate around z's grandparent.

As previously mentioned, fixInsert function is a method to fix the red–black tree violations after inserting a new node to the tree. Thus, we need to declare the insert method, and this is identical to the insert operation as in a Binary Search Tree (for more information, check Chapter 11 "Binary Search Tree").

Here we will declare three methods: main insert method, addAsLeftNode, and addAsRightNode.

```
private func addAsLeftNode(child: RBTreeNode, parent:
RBTreeNode) {
    parent.leftChild = child
    child.parent = parent
    child.color = .red
    fixInsert(node: child)
}

private func addAsRightNode(child: RBTreeNode, parent:
RBTreeNode) {
    parent.rightChild = child
    child.parent = parent
    child.color = .red
    fixInsert(node: child)
}
```

addAsLeftNode – Adds a child as a left node, sets the color to red, and fixes violation

addAsRightNode – Adds a child as a right node, sets the color to red, and fixes violation

Then we create the main insert method which will use the preceding declared methods.

```swift
private func insert(input: RBTreeNode, node: RBTreeNode) {
    guard let inputKey = input.key, let nodeKey = node.key
    else {
        return
    }
    if inputKey < nodeKey {
      guard let child = node.leftChild else {
        addAsLeftNode(child: input, parent: node)
        return
      }
      if child.isNullLeaf {
        addAsLeftNode(child: input, parent: node)
      } else {
        insert(input: input, node: child)
      }
    } else {
      guard let child = node.rightChild else {
        addAsRightNode(child: input, parent: node)
        return
      }
      if child.isNullLeaf {
        addAsRightNode(child: input, parent: node)
      } else {
        insert(input: input, node: child)
      }
    }
  }
```

The insertion is identical to the insert operation as in a BST; the main difference is that nil pointers are replaced with nullLeaf, and after each insert, we call the fixInsert method to fix the violations.

## Deletion

Deletion is also similar to a standard delete method in a BST, but here we need a helper function to fix violations after deletion. There might be case that the parent and child of the deleted node are red so we have two adjacent red nodes, or if we delete the root node, the root could be red or other properties might be violated. So to fix up these violations, we create fixDelete method which includes four cases.

```
private func fixDelete(node y: RBTreeNode) {
    var yTemp = y
    if y.isRootNode && y.color == .black {
        guard var siblingNode = y.siblingNode else {
            return
        }
        // Case 1: Sibling of y is red.
        if siblingNode.color == .red {
            //Change color
            siblingNode.color = .black
            if let yParent = y.parent {
                yParent.color = .red
                // Rotate
                if y.isRightNode {
                    rotate(node: yParent, direction: .right)
                } else {
                    rotate(node: yParent, direction: .left)
                }
```

```
            // Update sibling
            if let sibling = y.siblingNode {
                siblingNode = sibling
            }
        }
    }
}
// Case 2: Sibling of y is black with two black
   children.
if siblingNode.leftChild?.color == .black &&
siblingNode.rightChild?.color == .black {
    //Change color
    siblingNode.color = .red
    //Move black unit upward
    if let yParent = y.parent {
        fixDelete(node: yParent)
    }
} else {
    // Case 3.1: Sibling is black and with one
       black child to the left.
    if y.isLeftNode && siblingNode.rightChild?.
    color == .black {
        //Change color
        siblingNode.leftChild?.color = .black
        siblingNode.color = .red
        //Rotation to the right
        rotate(node: siblingNode, direction:
        .right)
        //Update the sibling of y
        if let sibling = y.siblingNode {
            siblingNode = sibling
        }
```

```
    } //Case 3.2: One black child to the left
    else if y.isRightNode && siblingNode.
    leftChild?.color == .black {
        //Change color
        siblingNode.rightChild?.color = .black
        siblingNode.color = .red
        //Rotation to the left
        rotate(node: siblingNode, direction: .left)
        //Update the sibling of y
        if let sibling = y.siblingNode {
            siblingNode = sibling
        }
    }
}
// Case 4: Sibling is black with red right child.
if let yParent = y.parent {
    siblingNode.color = yParent.color
    yParent.color = .black
    // Case a: y is left and sibling with red right
        child
    if y.isLeftNode {
        siblingNode.rightChild?.color = .black
        rotate(node: yParent, direction: .left)
    }
    // Case b: y is right and sibling with red left
        child
    else {
        siblingNode.leftChild?.color = .black
        rotate(node: yParent, direction: .right)
    }
```

```
            yTemp = root
        }
    }
    yTemp.color = .black
}
```

Inside this function, we have implemented four cases.

**Case 1**: The sibling of y is red, and we know that the sibling is the other child of y's parent. In this, the color of y's parent and y's sibling will be changed and then we rotate left around y's parent (Figure 12-6).

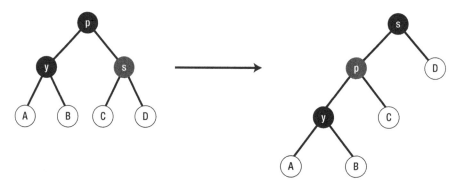

***Figure 12-6.*** *Case 1: y's sibling is red*

**Case 2**: y's sibling is black and it has two black children. In this case, we change the color of y's sibling to red and move y upward to y's parent and check again for this newY (Figure 12-7).

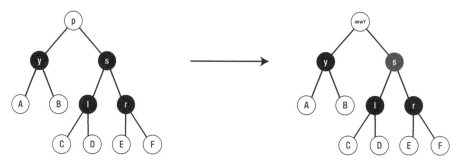

***Figure 12-7.*** *Case 2: y's sibling is black*

**Case 3**: y's sibling is black and it has one black child to the right. Here, we change the color of the sibling to red and sibling's left child to black and rotate around the sibling (Figure 12-8).

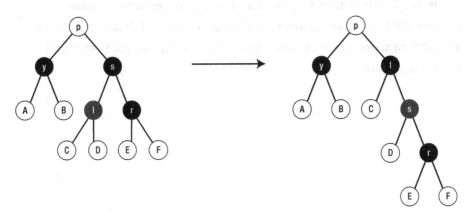

***Figure 12-8.***  *Case 3: y's sibling is black with black right child*

**Case 4**: y's sibling is black with red child to the right. In this case, we change the sibling's color to the y's parent and y's parent and sibling's right child to black and then rotate around y's parent (Figure 12-9).

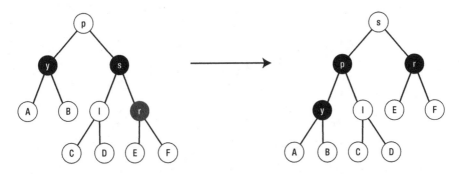

***Figure 12-9.***  *Case 4: y's sibling is black with red right child*

119

# Conclusion

In this chapter, you have learned about red–black tree and its main properties. Furthermore, you mastered how to implement various methods such as rotation, insert, and remove. The red–black tree is very powerful for worst-case scenarios when processing search, insert, and delete operations.

# CHAPTER 13

# Big O

To describe the efficiency of algorithms, Big O time language and metric is used. To make it clearer, let's look at the following scenario. Imagine that we want to send a file to our friend as fast as possible, how should we send it?

There are two options:

- Electronic transfer

- Physical delivery

## Time Complexity

The concept of asymptotic runtime or Big O means time complexity. Which means we could describe the data transfer algorithm runtime as follows (Figure 13-1):

- Electronic transfer: $O(s)$, where s is the size of the file. This means that the time to transfer the file increases linearly with the size of the file.

- Physical delivery: $O(1)$ – as the size increases, it will not take any longer.

© Elshad Karimov 2020
E. Karimov, *Data Structures and Algorithms in Swift*,
https://doi.org/10.1007/978-1-4842-5769-2_13

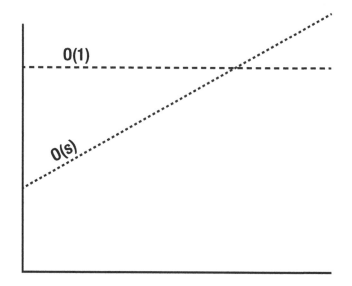

**Figure 13-1.** *Time complexity*

There are various types of runtime such as $O(N)$, $O(N^2)$, and $O(2^N)$. For instance, to paint an area of w meters wide and h meters high, the runtime could be described as $O(wh)$. Some algorithms are faster when the input is small; however, they become slower when the input gets larger. It is very crucial that our programs run fast, because they are not executed in supercomputers, so if a mobile app users face slow performance from the app, they tend to quit and delete the app. Thus, proper algorithm must be chosen for our development.

The runtime for any algorithm can be described in three different ways. As an example, let's examine a quick sort algorithm. It takes a random number element as a pivot and swaps values in the array before elements greater than the pivot appear (Figure 13-2).

- Best case: All elements are equal and pass over through an array happens once, $O(N)$.

- Worst case: If we are unlucky, the pivot is repeatedly the biggest element in the array, $O(N^2)$.

- Expected case: Sometimes the pivot will be very high or very low, but it will not happen over and over again, O(N log N).

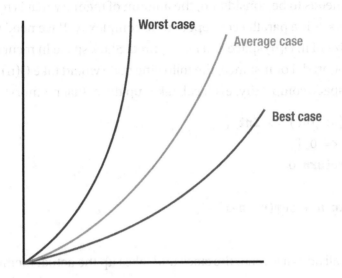

**Figure 13-2.** *Big O scenarios*

To express these cases, there are different Big O notations for them.

- Big-Theta (Big-Θ): It is a complexity that is within the bounds of the worst and the best cases.

- Big O: It is a complexity that is going to be less or equal to the worst case.

- Big-Omega (Big-Ω): It is a complexity that is going to be at least more than the best case.

# Space Complexity

When talking about the efficiency of an algorithm, time is not the only thing that needs to be considered, the amount of memory that is required also matters. It is a parallel concept to time complexity. If we need to create an array size of n, O(n) space will be required. Stack space in recursive calls are also counted. For instance, the following code would take O(n) time and O(n) space complexity; each call takes up the actual memory:

```
func sum(n: Int) -> Int {
    if n <= 0 {
        return 0
    }
    return n + sum(n: n-1)
}
```

Each call adds a level to the stack and takes up the actual memory:

```
1    sum(3)
2        → sum(2)
3            → sum(1)
4                → sum(0)
```

On the other hand, there are some cases that n calls do not take O(n) space:

```
func pairSumSequence(n: Int) -> Int {
    var sum = 0
    for i in 0...n {
        sum += pairSum(a: i, b: i+1)
    }
    return sum
}
```

```
func pairSum(a: Int, b: Int) -> Int {
    return a + b
}
```

Due to the fact that n calls to pairSum function do not exist simultaneously on the call stack, we only need O(1) space.

# Drop the Constants and Nondominant Terms

There is a possibility that O(N) code is faster than O(1) code for specific inputs. Big O just describes the rate of increase. So for this reason, we drop the constant which means that O(2N) is actually O(N).

- $O(2N) \rightarrow O(N)$

As we can drop constants, it is possible to drop nondominant terms.

- $O(N^2+N) \rightarrow O(N^2)$

- $O(N+logN) \rightarrow O(N)$

- $O(2*2^N + 1000N^{100}) \rightarrow O(2^N)$

Sometimes we might have a sum in the runtime, for example, $O(B^2+A)$ cannot be eliminated without the knowledge of A or B.

The following graph depicts the rate of increase for some common Big O times (Figure 13-3).

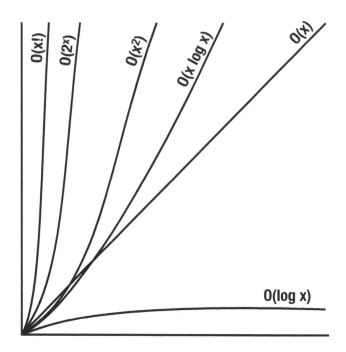

*Figure 13-3.* *Rate of increase for common Big O times*

As you can see, $O(x^2)$ is much worse than $O(x)$. There are a lot of runtimes that are worse than $O(x!)$ such as $O(x^x)$ or $O(2^x * x!)$.

# How to Calculate Complexities?

It is obvious that based on the code structure used in an algorithm, the complexity differs. Let's take a look at some code samples and their complexity.

- **If-else**: Inside this kind of blocks, normally we have two pieces of code – the code under **if** condition and the code under **else** condition. Here we take the worst-case condition. So, if the block if is $O(n)$ and the block else is $O(1)$, then the complexity for the entire block will be $O(n)$.

```
var myArray = [1,2,3,4,5]

if myArray.count > 0 {
    for i in myArray {
        print(i)
    }
} else {
    print("The array is empty")
}
```

From this code block, it can be easily seen that the complexity of **if** statement is O(n) and the complexity of **else** statement is O(1). However, the complexity for the entire code is O(n), because we always take into account the worst-case scenario.

- **Loops**: Inside the loop, the statements repeat themselves n times. If our code takes O(m) complexity to execute, inside n times repeated loop, it will be n*O(m) or O(n*m).

```
for i in myArray {
    print(i)
}
```

The number of loops will be 5 and the execution for the code inside the loop is O(1), so the combined execution will be O(5).

- **Nested** loops: If we have a loop inside another loop, the complexity will grow exponentially, which means that if complexity for a simple loop is O(n), the addition of another loop inside this loop will make the complexity O($n^2$).

```
for i in myArray {
    print(i)
    for a in myArray {
        print(i+a)
    }
}
```

Here the complexity for the first loop is O(5), because the array count is 5, so the nested loop also executed with the same complexity 5 times, and this means both will be O($5^2$).

# Add vs. Multiply

One of the main confusion is to find out when to add runtimes and when to multiply them.

- Adding runtimes – If an algorithm is in the form of "do this then when all done, do that"

- Multiplication – If an algorithm is in the form "do this for each time you do that"

On the left side, the runtime is O(A+B); this is because each runtime is run separately: first A is run and then B is run. Thus we add them together.

On the right side, we run B for each element of A, which means that we need to multiply the runtimes.

| Add the Runtimes: O(A+B) | Multiply the Runtimes: O(A*B) |
|---|---|
| ```
for a in arrayA {
  print(a)
}
for b in arrayB {
  print(b)
}
``` | ```
for a in arrayA {
  for b in arrayB {
      print("\(a) + \(b)")
  }
}
``` |

# Amortized Time

With an ArrayList or a dynamically resizing array, you won't run out of space since its capacity grows as you add elements. When the array hits the capacity, the ArrayList creates a new array with double capacity and copy all elements to the new array. So if the array contains N element, the runtime of adding elements will take O(N) time. We know that this does not happen very often and majority of the time adding will be O(1), and the amortized time takes into account both cases.

As we add elements, we double the capacity when the size of array is a power of 2. The capacity becomes 1,2,4,8,16 ... X. If we look at the sum of these capacities from the right to the left, it starts with X and halves until it gets 1.

X+X/2+X/4+X/8+...+1 and this is roughly 2X, and if we remove the constant, it becomes O(X). Therefore, X adds take O(X) time, and the amortized time for each adding is O(1).

# Log N Runtimes

If we look at the binary search as an example, in which we are looking for x in an N-element sorted array. First, we compare x to the midpoint – if it is equal, we return; if x<middle, then we search on the left; and if x>middle, we search on the right.

```
search 9 within [1,5,8,9,11,13,15,19,21]
    compare 9 to 11 → smaller
    search 9 within [1,5,8,9]
        compare 9 to 8 → bigger
        search 9 within [9]
            compare 9 to 9
            return
```

We start with N-element array search; then after single step, we are down to N/2 elements and one more step down to N/2 elements. So the total time is a matter of how many steps we can take until N becomes 1.

```
N = 16
N = 8 /* divide by 2 */
N = 4 /* divide by 2 */
N = 2 /* divide by 2 */
N = 1 /* divide by 2 */
```

So how many times can we multiply 1 by 2 to get N? $2^k = N \rightarrow \log_2 N = k$

Thus where the number of elements in the problem space gets halved each time, that will likely be a O(log N) runtime.

# Recursive Runtimes

What is the runtime of this code?

```swift
func f (n : Int) -> Int {
    if n <= 1 {
        return 1
    }
    return f(n: n-1) + f(n: n-1)
}
```

Rather than assumptions, let us look through the code. Suppose we have f(4) and this calls f(3) twice and each of those calls of f(3) calls f(2), until we get down to f(1) (Figure 13-4).

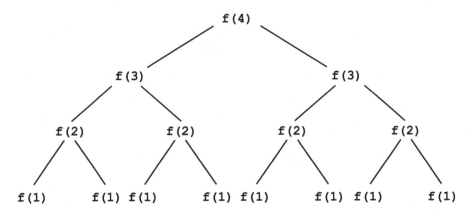

***Figure 13-4.*** *Recursive runtimes*

The tree will have depth N and each node has two children. Therefore, each level will have twice as many calls as the one shown in the figure. More generically it can be expressed as $2^0+2^1+2^2+2^3+...+2^{N-1}$. Thus, when you have a recursive function that makes multiple calls, the runtime will often look like O(branches$^{dept}$), but in our case, it is O($2^N$).

# Conclusion

In this chapter, you have learned about algorithm efficiency and how to measure it. We have identified the complexity of different codes. The time and space complexity have been explained and different types of complexities have been shown. In the next chapter, we are going to discuss the sorting algorithms.

# CHAPTER 14

# Sorting Algorithms

Until now we have covered different data structures and their performance. In this chapter, we will start learning about algorithms, which are the essential ways of processing data. The main functionality of algorithms is taking data as an input, processing it, and returning it as output.

In this chapter we will look at sorting algorithms which sort the data. The goal with sorting is to move from disarray to order. A sorting algorithm is made up of a series of instructions that takes lists as input, performs an operation on them, and outputs a sorted list. There are different types of sorting algorithms, but here we will discuss the following:

- Bubble sort

- Selection sort

- Insertion sort

- Merge sort

- Quick sort

## Bubble Sort

Bubble sort is an algorithm used to sort a sequence of numbers. It is used by starting at the beginning of a sequence and comparing the first couple elements. The elements are only swapped if the first element has a greater value than the second element. This process of comparing the adjacent elements continues throughout the array until the end has been reached

© Elshad Karimov 2020
E. Karimov, *Data Structures and Algorithms in Swift*,
https://doi.org/10.1007/978-1-4842-5769-2_14

and iterates again from the 0th index until the array has been sorted. It is a comparison-based algorithm that compares each pair of elements in an array and swaps them if they are out of order until the entire array is sorted. Refer to Figure 14-1. To sort this set of elements using the bubble sort algorithm, first, we compare 5 with 9 at the left end of the sequence. In this case, 5 is smaller than 9, which means that the numbers won't get swapped.

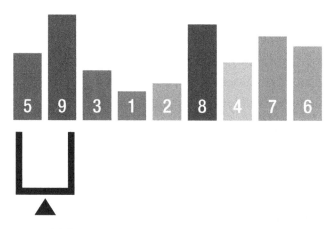

*Figure 14-1.* *Bubble sort comparison 1*

After the comparison is finished, the scales move one position to the right and the numbers are compared once again. This time 9 is greater than 3, so the numbers will be swapped, and the scale moves one position to the right (Figure 14-2).

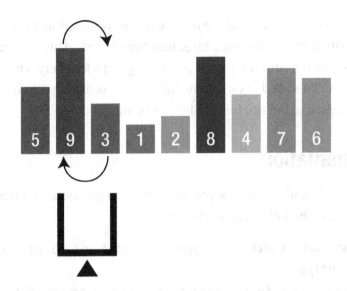

*Figure 14-2.* *Bubble sort comparison 2*

This operation is repeated until the scales reach the left end of the sequence. When the scales have reached the left end of the sequence, in one round of operation, the smallest value in the sequence has moved to the left edge and the number on the left edge is considered fully sorted. And the scales are moved back to the right edge, so the same operation is repeated until all of the numbers are fully sorted.

The bubble sort is very useful where we know the data is very nearly sorted. For example, if only two elements are out of place, then in one pass, bubble sort will finish sorting it, and in the second pass, it will see everything is sorted and then exit, which means that it takes only two passes of the array.

The primary advantage of the bubble sort is that it is popular and easy to implement. Furthermore, in the bubble sort, elements are swapped in place without using additional temporary storage, so the space requirement is at a minimum.

The main disadvantage of the bubble sort is the fact that it does not deal well with a list containing a huge number of items. This is because the bubble sort requires n-squared processing steps for every n number of elements to be sorted. As such, the bubble sort is mostly suitable for academic teaching but not for real-life applications.

# Implementation

Open up Xcode and create new playground file to get started for this chapter. Create the following function inside it:

```swift
public func bubbleSort<inputType : Comparable>(_ inputArray:
inout [inputType]) {
    for endofArray in (1..<inputArray.count).reversed() {
        var swapped = false
        for currentIndex in 0..<endofArray {
            if inputArray[currentIndex] >
            inputArray[currentIndex + 1] {
                inputArray.swapAt(currentIndex, currentIndex+1)
                swapped = true
            }
        }
        if !swapped {
            return
        }
    }
}
```

Inside the first loop with a single pass, the largest value goes to the end of the collection and then every pass needs to compare one less value than in the previous pass, so each time the array is shortened by one. The second loop compares the adjacent values, and if the current value is greater than the next value, it swaps them using the swapAt function.

Let's take a look at the following array:

```
var testArray = [9, 2, 6, 4, 5]
print("Initial array: \(testArray)")
bubbleSort(&testArray)
print("Sorted array: \(testArray)")
```

The output will be

**Initial array: [9, 2, 6, 4, 5]**
**Sorted array: [2, 4, 5, 6, 9]**

# Selection Sort

Selection sort is another sorting algorithm that is used to sort a sequence
of numbers. Using a linear search, the smallest value in the sequence
is located, and this value swaps with the leftmost number and it is
considered fully sorted. If the smallest value happens to already be in the
leftmost position, no operation is carried out. Then the same operations
are repeated until all of the numbers are fully sorted.

Let's assume that we have the following list of numbers (Figure 14-3).

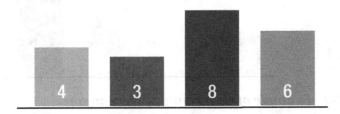

*Figure 14-3. Unsorted list for selection sort*

The selection sort works by repeatedly going through the list of items, each time selecting the lowest unsorted value and placing it in the correct position in the sequence as shown in Figure 14-4.

1. In this case, the lowest value is 3. It is swapped with 4 and 3 is considered sorted.

2. The next lowest value is 4 and we see that it is already in the right place.

3. The last lowest value is 6 and it is swapped with 8.

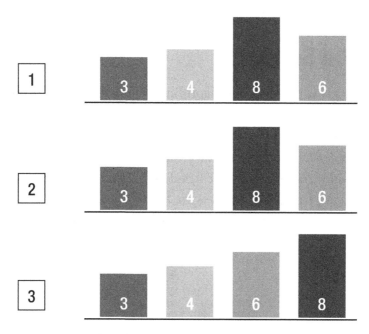

*Figure 14-4.  Example of performing a selection sort*

The main advantage of the selection sort is that it performs well on a small list. Furthermore, because it is an in-place sorting algorithm, no additional temporary storage is required beyond what is needed to hold the original list.

The primary disadvantage of the selection sort is its poor efficiency when dealing with a huge list of items. Similar to the bubble sort, the selection sort requires n-squared number of steps for sorting n elements. Additionally, its performance is easily influenced by the initial ordering of the items before the sorting process. Because of this, the selection sort is only suitable for a list of few elements that are in random order.

# Implementation

Let's create a selectionSort function as shown in the following code:

```
public func selectionSort<inputType: Comparable>(_ inputArray:
inout [inputType]) {
    for  currentIndex in 0..<(inputArray.count-1) {
        var lowestValueIndex = currentIndex
        for nextIndex in (currentIndex+1)..<inputArray.count {
            if inputArray[lowestValueIndex] >
            inputArray[nextIndex] {
                lowestValueIndex = nextIndex
            }
        }
        if lowestValueIndex != currentIndex {
            inputArray.swapAt(lowestValueIndex, currentIndex)
        }
    }
}
```

Inside the selectionSort function, we loop through all elements in the collection, except the last one. If all elements are sorted, there is no need to sort the last one. In the next loop, we find the lowest value in the list, and if that element is not the current element, we swap them.

Let's take a look at the following array:

```
var testArray = [9, 2, 6, 4, 5, 10, 8]
print("Initial array: \(testArray)")
selectionSort(&testArray)
print("Sorted array: \(testArray)")
```

The output will be

**Initial array: [9, 2, 6, 4, 5, 10, 8]**
**Sorted array: [2, 4, 5, 6, 8, 9, 10]**

It can be easily seen that selection sort performs better than bubble sort.

# Insertion Sort

Insertion sort is one of the most popular and simple sorting algorithms. The average time complexity of insertion sort is $O(n^2)$, which means that it is very inefficient for sorting larger datasets. Insertion sort can be used when the data is nearly sorted or when the dataset is small. In the mentioned conditions, the time complexity can be reached to $O(n \log(n))$.

In insertion sort when we begin, the leftmost number is considered fully sorted. Then from the remaining numbers, the leftmost number is taken out and compared to the already sorted number to its left, and if the already sorted number is larger, the two numbers swap. This operation repeats until either a number smaller appears or the number reaches to the left edge.

Let's assume that we have the following list of numbers (Figure 14-5).

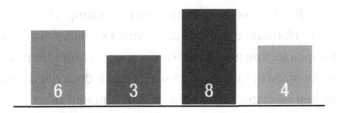

***Figure 14-5.*** *Unsorted list for insertion sort*

As shown in Figure 14-6, In this case 6 is greater than 3, so the numbers swap. And the number reaches to the left edge, so it stops there and considered fully sorted, and in our case 3 is now fully sorted. Then again the leftmost number from the remaining numbers is taken out and compared to the number to its left. Next, 6 is less than 8, so the numbers will be not be swapped, and 6 is considered fully sorted. Then 8 is taken out and compared with 4 and it is greater which means the numbers will be swapped, and we compare 4 with 6 and we see that 6 is greater than 4, so again the numbers will be swapped. When it reaches the number that is smaller, it stops there and considered fully sorted. Finally, since all the numbers are fully sorted, sorting is complete.

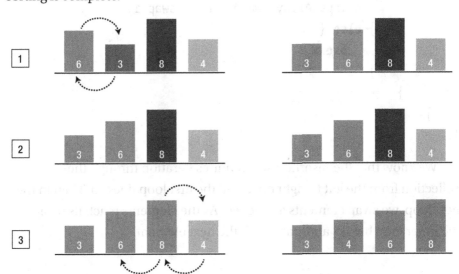

***Figure 14-6.*** *Insertion sort steps*

The main advantage of the insertion sort is its simplicity. It also exhibits good performance when dealing with a small list. The insertion sort is an in-place sorting algorithm, so the space requirement is minimal.

The disadvantage of the insertion sort is that it does not perform as well as other better sorting algorithms. With n-squared steps required for every n element to be sorted, the insertion sort does not deal well with a huge list. Therefore, the insertion sort is particularly useful when sorting a list of few items.

# Implementation

Let's create an insertion sort function as shown in the following code:

```swift
public func insertionSort<inputType: Comparable>(_ inputArray:
inout [inputType]) {
    for currentIndex in 1..<inputArray.count {
        for swap in (1...currentIndex).reversed() {
            if inputArray[swap] < inputArray[swap - 1] {
                inputArray.swapAt(swap, swap-1)
            } else {
                break
            }
        }
    }
}
```

We know that the insertion sort requires iteration through the collection from the left to right once and the first loop does so. Then in the next loop, we swap elements as needed. As the elements reach its position, the inner loop breaks and starts with the next element.

Let's take a look at the following array:

```
var testArray = [9, 2, 6, 4, 5, 10, 8, 12, 16, 11]
print("Initial array: \(testArray)")
insertionSort(&testArray)
print("Sorted array: \(testArray)")
```

The output will be

**Initial array: [9, 2, 6, 4, 5, 10, 8, 12, 16, 11]**
**Sorted array: [2, 4, 5, 6, 8, 9, 10, 11, 12, 16]**

The insertion sort is useful when you have a list that is mostly sorted. A card game would be a good example. When a player receives a new card, it is added to their existing hand and the insertion can efficiently resort the list of cards.

# Merge Sort

Merge sort is another sorting algorithm which has a lower-order running time than the insertion sort. It is a divide-and-conquer algorithm. Merge sort divides the sequence further and further into halves, and when the division is complete, the next thing it will do is combine the divided groups back. During the combination of divided groups, each group's number is arranged so that they are ordered from smallest to largest. When groups with multiple numbers are combined, the first numbers are compared first.

Let's assume that we have the following list of numbers (Figure 14-7).

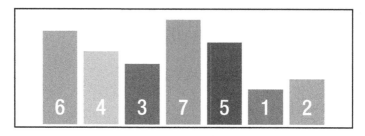

***Figure 14-7.*** *Unsorted list for merge sort*

The division will be as shown in Figure 14-8.

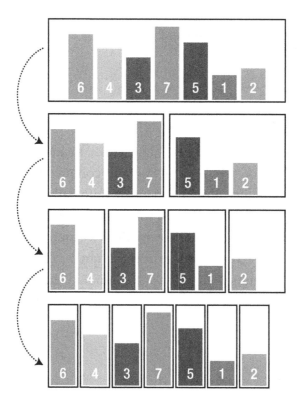

***Figure 14-8.*** *Merge sort divide*

It can be easily seen that in each step merge sort divides the sequence into halves. After the division is finished, the combination process starts, and while combining, the divided group elements are compared to be arranged in order (Figure 14-9).

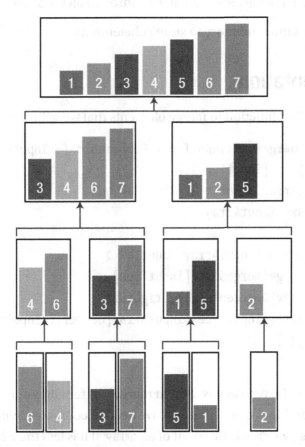

***Figure 14-9.*** *Merge sort combine*

Advantages

- It is quicker for larger lists because unlike insertion and bubble sort, it does not loop through the list.

- It has a consistent running time.

Disadvantages

- Slower for smaller lists compared to other sorting algorithms.

- Even if the list is sorted, it goes through all the steps.

- Uses more memory to store subelements.

# Implementation

We need another function to merge elements that we split.

```
public func mergeSort<inputType: Comparable>(_ inputArray:
[inputType]) -> [inputType] {
    if inputArray.count < 2 {
        return inputArray
    }
    let center = (inputArray.count) / 2
    return merge(mergeSort([inputType]
    (inputArray[0..<center])), rightList:
      mergeSort([inputType](inputArray[center..<inputArray.
      count])))
}
```

Here again the type that is used in mergeSort function must conform to the Comparable protocol, because we need to compare elements of the array. First, we check the count of an array; if it is less than 2, then it is considered sorted and the array itself is returned. Then we divide the list into two and call mergeSort function recursively.

Merge function:

```
private func merge<inputType: Comparable>(_ leftList:
[inputType], rightList: [inputType]) -> [inputType] {
    var leftIndex = 0
```

```
var rightIndex = 0
var tmpList = [inputType]()
tmpList.reserveCapacity(leftList.count + rightList.count)
while (leftIndex < leftList.count && rightIndex <
rightList.count) {
    if leftList[leftIndex] < rightList[rightIndex] {
        tmpList.append(leftList[leftIndex])
        leftIndex += 1
    } else if leftList[leftIndex] > rightList[rightIndex] {
        tmpList.append(rightList[rightIndex])
        rightIndex += 1
    } else {
        tmpList.append(leftList[leftIndex])
        tmpList.append(rightList[rightIndex])
        leftIndex += 1
        rightIndex += 1
    }
}

tmpList += [inputType](leftList[leftIndex..<leftList.
count])
tmpList += [inputType](rightList[rightIndex..<rightList.
count])
return tmpList
}
```

Merge function also conforms to Comparable protocol and it takes two lists as parameters. First we create a temporary array and reserve a capacity for it. Then by using the while loop, we loop through the lists until either the left or right index is equal to their respective sequence count. Then we start to compare the values from the left and right sequences; if the leftList element is less than the rightList, we add it to the temporary array and increment the leftIndex. If the leftList element is greater than the rightList, then we add the rightList element to the temporary array and increment the rightIndex; otherwise these elements are equal and we add the right and left elements and increment both indexes.

Let's take a look at the following array:

```
var testArray = [9, 2, 6, 4, 5, 10, 8, 12, 16, 11]
print("Initial array: \(testArray)")
print(mergeSort(testArray))
```

The output will be

**Initial array: [9, 2, 6, 4, 5, 10, 8, 12, 16, 11]**
**Result array: [2, 4, 5, 6, 8, 9, 10, 11, 12, 16]**

# Quick Sort

Quick sort is also a divide-and-conquer algorithm to sort the sequence. One of the main characteristics of Quick sort is that it involves fewer comparisons and swaps compared to other algorithms, so it is able to sort quickly in many cases. The algorithm works by partitioning an initial array into sublists based on a pivot element. All elements in the first sublist are arranged to be smaller than the pivot, while all elements in the second sublist are arranged to be larger than the pivot. The same partitioning and arranging process is performed repeatedly on the resulting sublists until the whole list of items is sorted. The average running time is O(n log n), due to its tight inner loop. In the worst-case scenario, its running time is o($n^2$).

Let's assume that we have the following list of numbers (Figure 14-10).

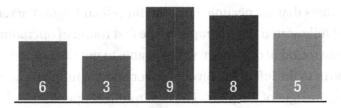

***Figure 14-10.***  *Unsorted list for quick sort*

The first operation in this unsorted list targets the entire sequence of numbers, and a number is chosen as a reference for sorting which is called pivot and it is chosen at random. This time, for convenience, let's choose the rightmost number as the pivot, which is 5. The next thing that we are going to do is to place a left marker on the leftmost number and a right marker on the rightmost number. Quick sort uses these markers to repeatedly perform rounds of operation recursively. The left marker moves to the right and, in each step, compares the number with the pivot number and stops when it reaches a number that is greater or equal to the pivot number. In our case it stops at 6 because it is greater than 5. Then the right marker starts to move to the left, and this time when it reaches a number that is less than the pivot number, in our case, it stops at 3 which is less than 5. When both the left and right markers have stopped, the markers' numbers are swapped; here we swap 3 with 6.

In this way the left marker acts to find numbers that are greater or equal to the pivot, and the right marker finds numbers less than the pivot, and by swapping these numbers, we can gather numbers that are less than the pivot on the left side of the sequence and numbers that are greater than or equal to the pivot on the right side.

Like before, the left marker moves until it reaches a number that is greater than or equal to the pivot number, which is 6 in our case. And once again the right marker moves to the left and the movement stops when the right marker runs into the left marker. When both the left and right markers stop in the same position, that number is swapped with the pivot number.

So the numbers that are occupied by both the left and right markers are considered fully sorted. This completes the first round of operations.

With one round of operation, we were able to put the numbers smaller than the pivot to the left of the pivot number and the numbers larger than the pivot to the right of the pivot. The next round of operations will be performed recursively on both sequences created by the division as shown in Figure 14-11.

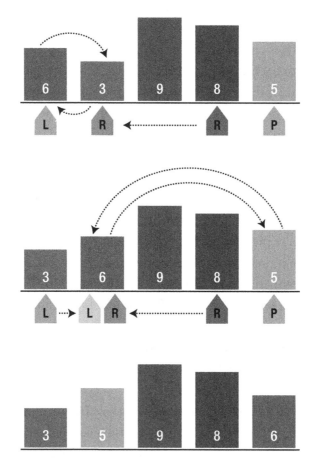

**Figure 14-11.** *Example of performing a quick sort*

The quick sort is regarded as the best sorting algorithm. This is because of its significant advantage in terms of efficiency because it is able to deal well with a huge list of items. Moreover, due to the fact that it sorts in a place, no additional storage is required as well.

The slight disadvantage of quick sort is that its worst-case performance is similar to the average performances of the bubble, insertion, or selection sort.

In general, the quick sort produces the most effective and widely used method of sorting a list of any item size.

# Implementation

Here again we need another helper function for pivot number.

```swift
func partition<inputType: Comparable>(_ inputArray: inout
[inputType], lowIndex: Int, hiIndex: Int) -> Int {
    let pivot = inputArray[hiIndex]
    var i = lowIndex

    for j in lowIndex..<hiIndex {
        if inputArray[j] <= pivot {
            inputArray.swapAt(i, j)
            i += 1
        }
    }

    inputArray.swapAt(i, hiIndex)
    return i
}
```

The purpose of the partition function is to select the pivot number and to sort sublists. First, we choose the rightmost number as a pivot number and create new variable and assign lowIndex value to it. Then we iterate through our array comparing each element with the pivot number. If the current element is less than the pivot value, we swap it with the current position of i, which starts from lowIndex, and increment each when a swap occurs. By doing it repeatedly, we push the larger elements to the right and the smaller elements to the left. At the end, after the iteration is completed, we swap the i and hi elements, which moves our pivot element back in place and returns i value as pivot number.

Quick sort function: It calls the partition function and recursively itself to sort subsequences of the array.

```swift
func quickSort<inputType: Comparable>(_ inputArray: inout
[inputType], lowIndex: Int, hiIndex: Int) {
    if lowIndex < hiIndex {
      let pivot = partition(&inputArray, lowIndex: lowIndex,
      hiIndex: hiIndex)
        quickSort(&inputArray, lowIndex: lowIndex, hiIndex:
        pivot - 1)
        quickSort(&inputArray, lowIndex: pivot + 1, hiIndex:
        hiIndex)
    }
}
```

## Pivot Selection

Selection of the rightmost number as the pivot number as we did here can have a negative impact on the performance. If the array is already sorted, it will produce the worst-case scenario $O(n^2)$, and selection of random value does not guarantee that it will select the best value. So what is the best approach to select pivot number?

The best approach is a median-of-three strategy. Here we take the median of the lowest, center, and highest numbers. To implement it, we need another helper function which helps us to get the median of the three values.

```swift
private func getMedian<inputType: Comparable>(_ inputArray:
inout [inputType], lowIndex: Int, hiIndex: Int) -> inputType {
    let center = lowIndex + (hiIndex - lowIndex) / 2
    if inputArray[lowIndex] > inputArray[center] {
        inputArray.swapAt(lowIndex, center)
    }

    if inputArray[lowIndex] > inputArray[hiIndex] {
        inputArray.swapAt(lowIndex, hiIndex)
    }

    if inputArray[center] > inputArray[hiIndex] {
        inputArray.swapAt(lowIndex, hiIndex)
    }

    inputArray.swapAt(center, hiIndex)

    return inputArray[hiIndex]
}
```

We can use this function inside the partition function to pass the
median value for it.

# Conclusion

In this chapter, you have learned about some sorting algorithms and
strategies behind them. You mastered about bubble sort, selection sort,
insertion sort, merge sort, and quick sort and their advantages and
disadvantages. By now you should have a good understanding of how
to implement these algorithms and which one to choose based on the
requirements. In the next chapter, we are going to learn about search
algorithms such as linear search and binary search.

# CHAPTER 15

# Search Algorithms

To check for an element or retrieve an element from any data structure, searching algorithms are used. The performance of these algorithms is evaluated on how fast they can find a solution, and in most cases, this depends on the data structure being searched. Some data structures are specially designed to make search algorithms faster or more efficient.

Based on the mechanism of searching, search algorithms are classified into two categories:

- Sequential search: Linear search
- Interval search: Binary search

## Linear Search

Every element is checked sequentially for a searched value. When there are a lot of data, the number of comparisons increases, and it takes more time. The time complexity for linear search is O(n).

Let's look at following list (Figure 15-1).

***Figure 15-1.*** *List*

© Elshad Karimov 2020
E. Karimov, *Data Structures and Algorithms in Swift*,
https://doi.org/10.1007/978-1-4842-5769-2_15

Let's try searching for number 7. First, we examine the leftmost number in the array. We compare it with 5, and if it matches, the search ends. If it does not match, we examine the next number to the right. We repeat the comparison until 7 is found. When we found 7, the search ends here (Figure 15-2).

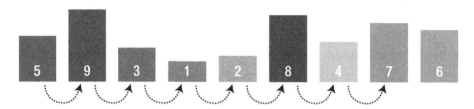

*Figure 15-2.* *Linear search*

The primary advantage of linear search is its simplicity: conceptually, it's extraordinarily easy to understand, and implementation-wise, it's also very straightforward. From an operational standpoint, linear search is also very resource efficient – it does not require copying/partitioning of the array being search – and thus it is memory efficient. It also operates equally well on both unsorted and sorted data.

The primary disadvantage of linear search is that it has a very poor O(n) general efficiency. That is, the performance of the algorithm scales linearly with the size of the input. For the general case, linear search thus is considerably slower than many other search algorithms.

In certain cases, where additional information about the current contents of the list being searched are known, linear search can perform as good or better than many other types of search algorithms. For instance, if you can assume that the list you have is a FIFO or LIFO, and you know that the item you are looking for is either almost always recently added or almost always at the end of the list, then a tailored linear search can provide a very good performance.

# Implementation

The linear search function is created using generics to make it compatible for all data types.

```
func linearSeacrh<inputType : Comparable>(_ inputArray:
[inputType], searchValue: inputType) -> String {
    let n = inputArray.count

    for i in 0..<n {
        if inputArray[i] == searchValue {
            return "The element is found at index \(i) "
        }
    }
    return "The element is not found"
}
```

First we take the length of the array and loop through it to search for the value, and when it is found, we return its index in the array. As you can see, the implementation is very easy to execute.

For example:

```
var testArray = [1,2,3,4,5,6]
print(linearSeacrh(testArray, searchValue: 6))
```

The output will be

**The element is found at index 5**

# Binary Search

Binary search is an algorithm for searching through the elements of a presorted array. It searches a sorted array by repeatedly dividing the search interval in half. First, it compares the searched value to the middle element of the array, and if the value of the search key is less than the item in the middle of the interval, it narrows the interval to the lower half. Otherwise, it narrows to the upper half and repeatedly checks until the value is found or the interval is empty. The worst-case time complexity for binary search is O(logN).

Binary search is faster than linear search except for small arrays, but the array must be sorted first to be able to apply binary search. It can be used to solve a wide range of problems, such as finding the smallest or next largest element in the array.

Let's look at the following list and use binary search for finding an element (Figure 15-3).

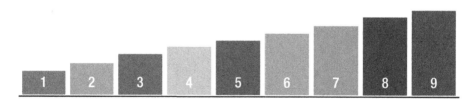

***Figure 15-3.*** *Sorted list*

Let's try searching for number 6 (Figure 15-4).

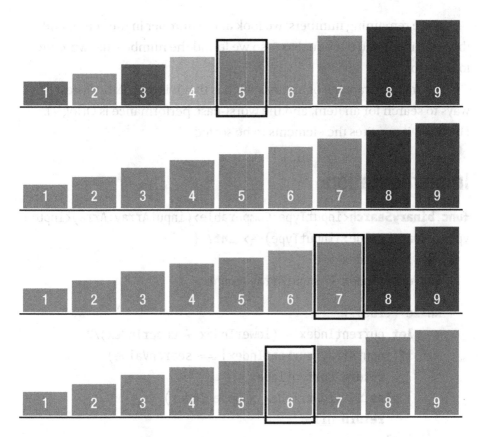

**Figure 15-4.** *Binary search*

First, we look at the number in the center of the array. In our case, it is 5 and we compare 5 to number 6 that we are searching for. And we see that 5 is less than 6, which means that number 6 is located at the right of 5 because we are looking into a pre-ordered array. So we remove the numbers that are no longer needed.

In the remaining numbers, again we look at the number in the center of the remaining array and this time it is 7. We compare 7 to 6 and it is greater than 6, which means that the number that we are looking for is located at the left of 7. Again we remove the numbers that we do not need.

In the remaining numbers, we look at the number in the center and this time it is 6 and 6 is equal to 6, so we found the number that we were looking for.

The main advantage of binary search is that it is one of the fastest ways to search for an item, and the worst-case performance is O(logN). However, it requires the elements to be sorted.

# Implementation

```swift
func binarySearch<inputType:Comparable>(inputArray:Array<inputType>, searchValue: inputType) -> Int? {
    var lowerIndex = 0
    var upperIndex = inputArray.count - 1

    while (true) {
        let currentIndex = (lowerIndex + upperIndex)/2
        if(inputArray[currentIndex] == searchValue) {
            return currentIndex
        } else if (lowerIndex > upperIndex) {
            return nil
        } else {
            if (inputArray[currentIndex] > searchValue) {
                upperIndex = currentIndex - 1
            } else {
                lowerIndex = currentIndex + 1
            }
        }
    }
}
```

First, we define the lower and upper indexes and loop through it to search for the value, by dividing the current list into two until the searched value is reached.

For example:

```
var testArray = [1,2,3,4,5,6,7,9,10];
if let searchIndex = binarySearch(inputArray:
testArray,searchValue: 5) {
    print("The element is found at index: \(searchIndex)")
}
```

The output will be

**The element is found at index: 4**

# Conclusion

In this chapter, you have learned about search algorithms and strategies behind them. You mastered about linear search and binary search and their advantages and disadvantages. By now you should have a good understanding of how to implement these algorithms and which one to choose based on the requirements. In the next chapter, we are going to learn about graph algorithms such as breadth-first search, depth-first search, and Dijkstra's algorithm.

# CHAPTER 16

# Graph Algorithms

It is obvious that the main purpose of many algorithms relates with operations on data, and the data structure plays an important role in choosing an algorithm. In this chapter, we will discuss nonlinear data structures such as graphs.

Graphs are nonlinear data structure which consist of nodes and edges. The basic structure of a graph is shown in Figure 16-1.

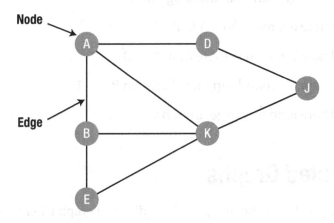

***Figure 16-1.*** *Graph data structure*

In the preceding graph, the set of nodes N = {A,B,D,E,K,J} and the set of edges E = {AB,AK, BK,BE,KJ,DJ}.

Graphs can be directed and undirected and the edges of graphs can have weights.

© Elshad Karimov 2020
E. Karimov, *Data Structures and Algorithms in Swift*,
https://doi.org/10.1007/978-1-4842-5769-2_16

# Directed Graphs

This type of graph is restrictive to traverse, as an edge may only permit traversal in one direction (Figure 16-2).

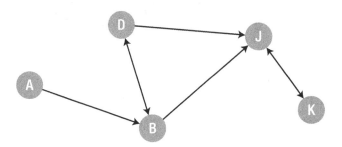

*Figure 16-2.* *Directed graph*

It can be easily seen from this diagram that

- There is a route from A to B

- There is no direct route from A to D

- There is a round trip route between B and D

- There is no way to get from B to A

# Undirected Graphs

Undirected graphs can be thought of as a directed graph where all edges are bidirectional (Figure 16-3).

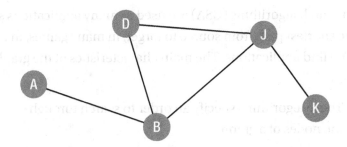

***Figure 16-3.*** *Undirected graph*

Here there are two routes back and forth and the weight of an edge applies to both ways.

# Weighted Graphs

The cost of using each edge is associated with a weight that is assigned to the edge. This makes easy to choose the cheapest path between edges (Figure 16-4).

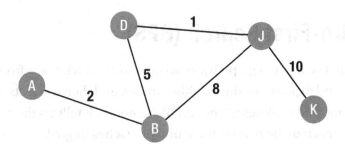

***Figure 16-4.*** *Weighted graph*

Graph search algorithms (GSA) are used in many applications such as finding the shortest path from source to target, in many games, in maps, and in route find applications. The main characteristics of the graph search are as follows:

- These algorithms specify an order to search through the nodes of a graph.

- We start at the source node and keep searching until we find the target node.

- The frontier contains nodes that we've seen but haven't explored yet.

- In each iteration, we take a node off the frontier and add its neighbors to the frontier.

There are many graph search algorithms, but here we will discuss only three of them: breadth-first search (BFS), depth-first search (DFS), and Dijkstra's algorithm.

# Breadth-First Search (BFS)

Breadth-first search is a graph traversal algorithm which starts from the root node and explores all the neighbor nodes, and then it selects the nearest node and explores all the rest of the nodes. It follows the same process for each of the nearest node until it reaches its goal.

Let's imagine that our goal in the following graph data structure is to find G using BFS (Figure 16-5).

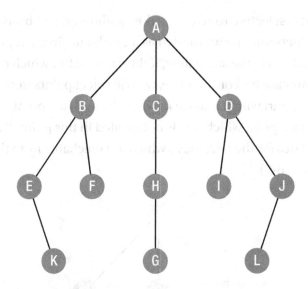

**Figure 16-5.** *Graph data structure*

The process starts with the search with A as the starting point. Points B, C, and D are reachable from A, and these are considered as candidates for the next point to move (Figure 16-6).

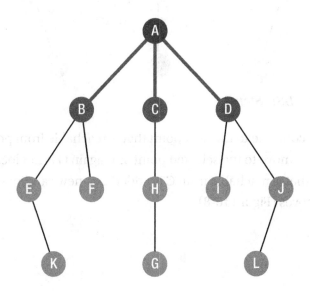

**Figure 16-6.** *BFS, Step 1*

One point is selected from among the candidates. The basis for selection is whichever one was added as a candidate first. For points that became candidates at the same time, it does not matter which one is selected. In our case for convenience, we will select points from the left side. So we will start with B and we move to the selected point and find out that the searched point which is G is not located in this point. E and F are added candidates for the next move which are reachable from the current point B (Figure 16-7).

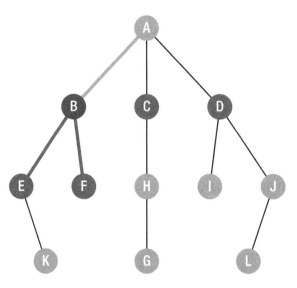

**Figure 16-7.**  *BSF, Step 2*

Then we continue to the next point that is reachable from point A, which is C. We move to the selected point and again G is not located here, so the point that is reachable from C is added as a new candidate for upcoming moves (Figure 16-8).

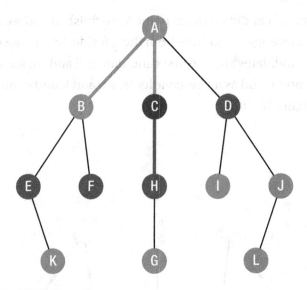

**Figure 16-8.** *BSF, Step 3*

Then we continue to the next point which is D and again G is not located here and I and J are added as new candidates (Figure 16-9).

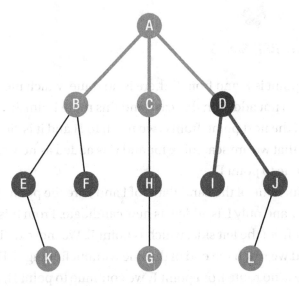

**Figure 16-9.** *BSF, Step 4*

We see that all candidates from point A are finished and we could not find point G, so we again continue from the left side. So we move from point B to its candidates and the first candidate is E and we see that G is not in this location, and as a new candidate, we add K and continue to the next point (Figure 16-10).

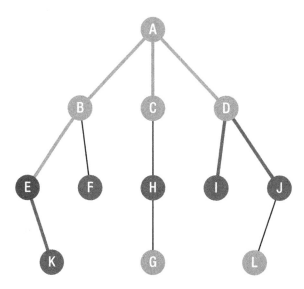

***Figure 16-10.*** *BSF, Step 5*

The next point is F, and from F, there is no route, which means that the candidate is not added in this case and this route is finished. Then, we continue with the next point, from C we reach to H and it is clear that H is not the point that we are searching for and G is added as new candidate and we continue to point D.

Here again, none of the candidates of I and J are the points that we are looking for and only L is added as new candidate. From this point, we again start from the left side, which is point E. We move to the next candidate and we reach the end of the line without finding G. Due to the fact that there is no route from point F, we continue to point H, and finally, when we move from H, we reach our goal, so the search ends here.

As you can see, the breadth-first search is unique in how it searches broadly from those points closest to the starting point.

Advantages of BFS

- If there is a solution, it will be found out by BFS.

- It will never get trapped in blind alley.

- If there is more than one solution, the solution will be found with minimal steps.

Disadvantages of BFS

- Memory constraint.

- If the solution is far away, it consumes more time.

# Implementation

In order to create a BFS algorithm, the following information must be included in the structure that will be declared:

- Node value

- The list of neighbors

- Visit status

So let's create a node class with these mentioned conditions.

```
public class BFSNode<T> {
    public var nodeValue:T
    public var nodeNeighbors:[BFSNode]
    public var visitedNode:Bool

    public init(value:T, neighbors:[BFSNode], visited:Bool) {
        self.nodeValue = value
        self.nodeNeighbors = neighbors
        self.visitedNode = visited
    }
}
```

```swift
    public func addNeighbor(node: BFSNode) {
        self.nodeNeighbors.append(node)
        node.nodeNeighbors.append(self)
    }

}
```

We also declared a method called addNeighbor to connect nodes.

To keep track of neighbors and visit status, we need additional data structure, a queue which is a FIFO data structure. When we start the search process with BFS, we will append queue by adding all neighbors to it, and as we visit them, they will be popped out one by one and marked as visited.

Let's add the following method to our BFSNode class:

```swift
public static func breadthFirstSearch(first:BFSNode) {
        var queue:[BFSNode] = []
        queue.append(first)

        while queue.isEmpty == false {
            if let node = queue.first {
                print(node.nodeValue)
                node.visitedNode = true
                for child in node.nodeNeighbors {
                    if child.visitedNode == false {
                        queue.append(child)
                    }
                }
                queue.removeFirst()
            }
        }
    }
```

First we initialize a queue that is composed of BFSNode and then append it with the first element. Then, inside the loop, we start visiting nodes in the queue, and as we visit the nodes, we mark them as visited and add not visited nodes to the queue. Finally, the processed nodes are removed and keep working with the rest of the queue.

For example:

```
let nodeA = BFSNode(value: "A", neighbors: [], visited: false)
let nodeB = BFSNode(value: "B", neighbors: [], visited: false)
let nodeC = BFSNode(value: "C", neighbors: [], visited: false)
let nodeD = BFSNode(value: "D", neighbors: [], visited: false)
let nodeE = BFSNode(value: "E", neighbors: [], visited: false)
let nodeF = BFSNode(value: "F", neighbors: [], visited: false)

nodeA.addNeighbor(node: nodeB)
nodeC.addNeighbor(node: nodeB)
nodeD.addNeighbor(node: nodeB)
nodeE.addNeighbor(node: nodeB)
nodeF.addNeighbor(node: nodeD)

BFSNode.breadthFirstSearch(first: nodeA)
```

The output will be

**A**
**B**
**C**
**D**
**E**
**F**

It can be easily seen that we search the graph in BFS style, by visiting each level's child before going deeper.

# Depth-First Search (DFS)

Depth-first search (DFS) is a recursive algorithm that explores a branch as far as possible until it reaches the end. When it reaches the end of the branch, it moves a step back and explores the next available branch until it finds the value that we are looking for. To avoid visiting a node more than once, a Boolean value is used for tracking.

Let's look at the following example:

Our goal is to find G by using DFS (Figure 16-11).

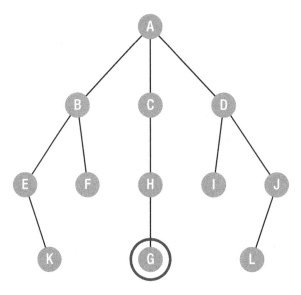

***Figure 16-11.*** *We're going to look for G using a depth-first search*

The beginning point is A; from this point, B, C, and D are reachable and they will be considered as candidates for the next point to move to (Figure 16-12).

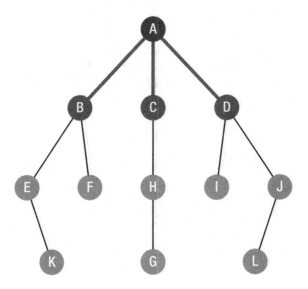

***Figure 16-12.*** *DFS, Step 1*

Then we select one point among the candidates and the basis for selection is whichever one was added as a candidate last. For the points that became candidates at the same time, it does not matter which one is selected. We start to select from the left side; in our case, it is B and we move to the selected point. Points E and F are reachable from point B, so they are added as new candidates for the next move (Figure 16-13).

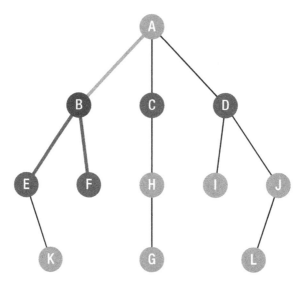

**Figure 16-13.** *DFS, Step 2*

Here again we have two new candidates which are added at the same time, so we select the one which is on the left which is E and we move to the selected point and the reachable point K is added as the new candidate. Please notice that in depth-first search we are not going back to the point which is reachable from A as in breadth-first search; here we continue until the end of reachable points (Figure 16-14).

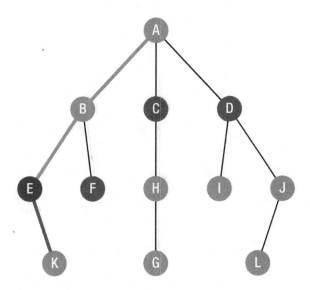

***Figure 16-14.*** *DFS, Step 3*

The next point that we will go is K, and from here there is no point that can be reached. So we continue to the next point that is reachable from B, and here again there is no point to go and the value that we are searching for is not located in this path. Thus, we will continue to the next point that is reachable from A. We move to C, and H is added as the new candidate (Figure 16-15).

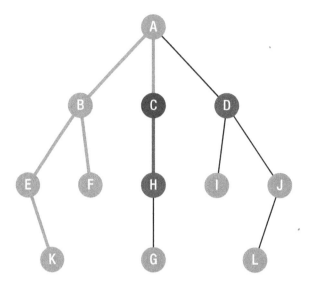

**Figure 16-15.** *DFS, Step 4*

And in the next stage, we move to H. When we reach here, G is added as the new candidate, and in the next step we move there. Finally, our goal is reached, so the search is ended here (Figure 16-16).

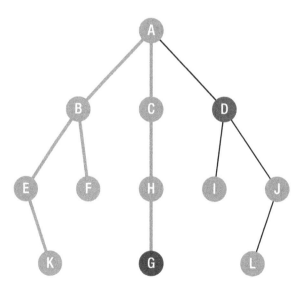

**Figure 16-16.** *DSF, Step 5*

As you can see, the depth-first search is unique in how it searches by digging more into a particular path. We have Binary Search Tree, as we start at the root: node with value A. Step 2 visits the first child (from left to right), which is the node with value B. Then, as this node has children too, we have to visit them first (again, from left to right): so in Step 3, we are visiting the node with value E. The search process continues until it reaches the goal.

Advantages

- Memory requirement is linear.

- Less time and space complexity.

- Solution can be found without much more search.

Disadvantages

- Solution is not guaranteed.

- It might be trapped in searching useless path.

# Implementation

First we will create a Tree Node which consists of value and children. The init method is also included here because Swift requires to create init method manually for classes. Then we add the addChild function to assign a child to a given node.

```
public class DFNode<inputType> {
    public var value: inputType
    public var children: [DFNode] = []

    public init(_ value: inputType) {
        self.value = value
    }
```

```
    public func addChild(_ child: DFNode) {
        children.append(child)
    }

}
```

We use the Tree Node inside the DFS. To do so we create another function inside the Tree Node class which uses recursion process in the next node.

```
public func depthFirstSearch(visit: (DFNode) -> Void) {
        visit(self)
        children.forEach {
            $0.depthFirstSearch(visit: visit)
        }
    }
```

For example:

Firstly, we create a tree node and add children to it; then we will use the depthFirstSearch function to show how it works.

```
let nodeA = DFNode("A")
let nodeB = DFNode("B")
let nodeC = DFNode("C")
let nodeD = DFNode("D")
let nodeE = DFNode("E")
let nodeF = DFNode("F")
let nodeG = DFNode("G")

nodeA.addChild(nodeB)
nodeA.addChild(nodeC)
nodeB.addChild(nodeE)
nodeB.addChild(nodeF)
nodeE.addChild(nodeG)
```

The tree that we created here is visually shown in Figure 16-17.

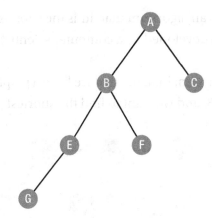

***Figure 16-17.*** *DFS example*

If we run the depthFirsthSearch method for this tree, the output will be

```
nodeA.depthFirstSearch {
    print($0.value)
}
```

Output:

```
A
B
E
G
F
C
```

It can be easily seen that we search the graph in DFS style, by visiting deeper before going to other children.

# Dijkstra's Algorithm

Dijkstra's algorithm is an algorithm that finds the shortest path between points in a graph. It is developed by a computer scientist Edsger w. Dijkstra in 1956.

Let's look at it in action; imagine that we have a graph data structure as shown in Figure 16-18, and we want to find the shortest path from A to G.

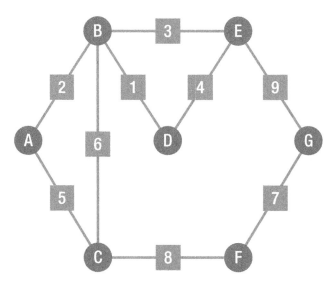

***Figure 16-18.*** *Graph for Dijkstra's algorithm*

It can be easily seen from the graph that the cost is available for all paths. In Step 1, the starting point is set to 0 and all other points are set to infinity. We start from the first point and search for unexplored points, and once these points are found, they become candidates for moving to the next (Figure 16-19).

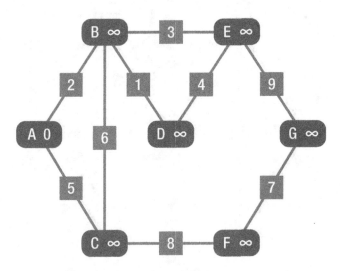

***Figure 16-19.*** *Dijkstra's algorithm, Step 1*

Step 2: At this stage, points B and C are our candidates, and the cost for each point is calculated based on the current point's cost plus the cost of moving to a candidate point. In our case the cost of A is 0 and moving to B is 2; the cost of B will be 0+2 = 2. Similarly, the cost of moving to C will be 0+5=5. So if the calculated cost is less than the current value, the point's cost is updated to the new value. Since the current costs of B and C are infinity, the calculated results are less, so B and C are updated to the new values (Figure 16-20).

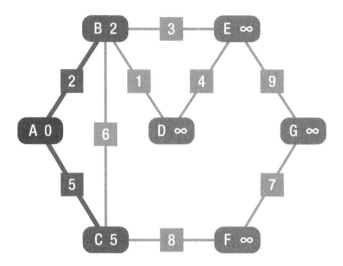

**Figure 16-20.** *Dijkstra's algorithm, Step 2*

Step 3: At this stage, we need to choose the next point to move to, and the one with the lowest cost is chosen which is B in this case. This means that A → B is the shortest path from the starting point to B. Taking the path determined to be the shortest, we move to point B and there are three candidates in this point, so C, D, and E are added as the new candidates. Using the cost calculation method, we calculate the cost of each candidate (Figure 16-21).

> B → C : 2 + 6 = 8, which is greater than C's current value of 5, so no update is made.
>
> B → D : 2 + 1 = 3, which is less than D's current value of infinity, so the value is updated.
>
> B → E : 2 + 3 = 5, which is less than E's current value of infinity, so the value is updated.

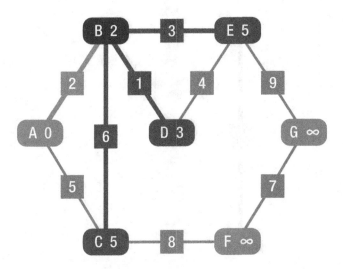

***Figure 16-21.*** *Dijkstra's algorithm, Step 3*

Step 4: Here again we choose the point with the lowest cost which is D. At this point we have determined that the chosen A → B → D is the shortest path from starting point A to D, so we move to point D. There is one candidate in this point, so E is added as the new candidate and the cost of E is calculated (Figure 16-22).

D → E : 3 + 4 = 7, which is greater than E's current value of 5, so no update is made.

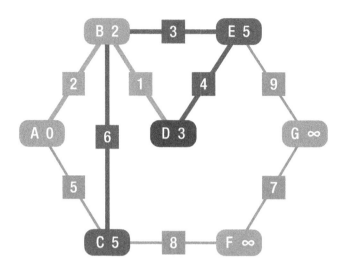

**Figure 16-22.** *Dijkstra's algorithm, Step 4*

Step 5: The cost to E from D is not the lowest cost, the cost of point C is lower than E and it is minimum with a value of 5, and that is why our next move is C. There is one candidate in this point, so F is added as the new candidate and the cost of F is calculated (Figure 16-23).

$C \rightarrow F : 5 + 8 = 13$, which is less than F's current value of infinity, so the value is updated.

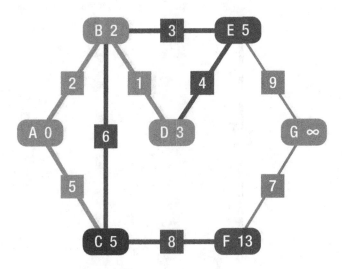

**Figure 16-23.** *Dijkstra's algorithm, Step 5*

Step 6: The cost of F is greater than the cost of E, so the lowest cost point is E with a value of 5. We move to E and there is only one candidate from this point which is G; it is added as the new candidate and the cost is calculated (Figure 16-24).

> E → G : 5 + 9 = 14, which is less than G's current
> value of infinity, so the value is updated.

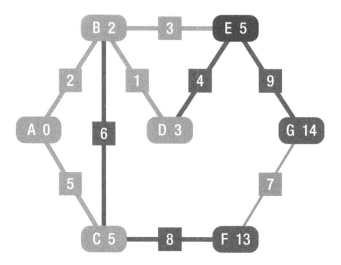

**Figure 16-24.** *Dijkstra's algorithm, Step 6*

Step 7: The cost of F is lower than G. We move to F and there is only one candidate from this point which is G; it is added as the new candidate and the cost is calculated (Figure 16-25).

> F → G : 13 + 7 = 20, which is greater than G's current
> value of 14, no update is made.

This means that E → G is better than F → G path and finally we reach our goal, and the beast way is A → B → E → G with the cost of 14.

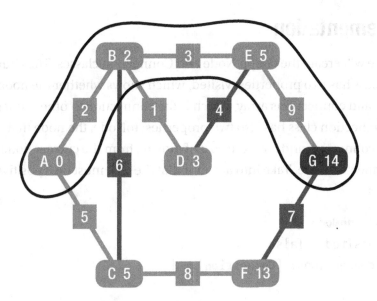

**Figure 16-25.** *Dijkstra's algorithm, Step 7*

As you can see, Dijkstra's algorithm efficiently searches for the shortest path by devising which point to choose next.

Advantages

- It is used in maps.

- Distance between the location refers to the edges.

- It is used in telephone network.

Disadvantages

- It does blind search which is a waste of time.

- It cannot handle negative edges.

# Implementation

First, we will create the Graph Node and Connection classes. The Graph Node class has two properties: visited, which shows whether the node is visited, and connections array, which is the connection to other nodes. The Connection class has also two properties: toNode, the node that will be connected, and cost, the cost of moving from the current node to the connected node. Take into account that the cost must be a positive number.

```swift
class GraphNode {
  var visited = false
  var connections: [Connection] = []
}

class Connection {
  public let toNode: GraphNode
  public let cost: Int

  public init(to node: GraphNode, cost: Int) {
    assert(cost >= 0, "Cost has to be equal or greater than
    zero")
    self.toNode = node
    self.cost = cost
  }
}
```

Then we need to create another class for the path. The purpose of this class is to keep track of paths that we have already visited and how we got there, and it will be used to describe the shortest path for our goal.

```swift
class Path {
    public let cumulativeCost: Int
    public let node: GraphNode
    public let previousPath: Path?
```

```
init(to node: GraphNode, via connection: Connection? = nil,
previousPath path: Path? = nil) {
    if let previousPath = path, let viaConnection =
    connection {
      self.cumulativeCost = viaConnection.cost +
      previousPath.cumulativeCost
    } else {
      self.cumulativeCost = 0
    }
    self.node = node
    self.previousPath = path
  }
}
```

Here we declared another property called cumulativeCost to keep track of the cost for reaching to the current point. This is the sum of all the connections cost that we have travelled from the source node to this node.

# Algorithm

Firstly, we define the path collection which consists of nodes that can reach from the nodes that we have visited so far. Initially it is empty; then we append it with paths to source the node. After appending the paths, the first step that we are going to do is to extract the cheapest path from the path collection and check if the node has not been visited yet, and then we proceed to the next step. Then we check whether we reach our destination, and if so, we return the cheapest path in the path collection (**return** cheapestPathInPathCollection). If we do not reach our destination, we mark the current node as visited (cheapestPathInPathCollection.node. visited = true). Then inside the **for** loop, we add new candidates which are reachable from the current node. In this way, Dijkstra's algorithm finds the cheapest way to our destination.

```swift
func dijskastraShortestPath(source: GraphNode, destination:
GraphNode) -> Path? {
    var pathCollection: [Path] = [] {
        didSet {
            pathCollection.sort { return $0.cumulativeCost <
            $1.cumulativeCost }
        }
    }

    pathCollection.append(Path(to: source))
    while !pathCollection.isEmpty {
        let cheapestPathInPathCollection = pathCollection.
        removeFirst()
        guard !cheapestPathInPathCollection.node.visited else {
        continue }

        if cheapestPathInPathCollection.node === destination {
            return cheapestPathInPathCollection
        }

        cheapestPathInPathCollection.node.visited = true

        for connection in cheapestPathInPathCollection.node.
        connections where !connection.toNode.visited {
            pathCollection.append(Path(to: connection.
            toNode, via: connection, previousPath:
            cheapestPathInPathCollection))
        }
    }
    return nil
}
```

For example:

Let's create the preceding illustrated graph and find the cheapest way to our goal to find the shortest path to point G from point A.

Step 1: Create the custom class which conforms to our GraphNode class.

```
class sampleGraphNode: GraphNode {
  let name: String

  init(name: String) {
    self.name = name
    super.init()
  }
}
```

Step 2: Create nodes based on sampleGraphNode.

```
let nodeA = sampleGraphNode(name: "A")
let nodeB = sampleGraphNode(name: "B")
let nodeC = sampleGraphNode(name: "C")
let nodeD = sampleGraphNode(name: "D")
let nodeE = sampleGraphNode(name: "E")
let nodeF = sampleGraphNode(name: "F")
let nodeG = sampleGraphNode(name: "G")
```

Step 3: Create connection between these nodes and assign cost to these paths.

```
nodeA.connections.append(Connection(to: nodeB, cost: 2))
nodeA.connections.append(Connection(to: nodeC, cost: 5))
nodeB.connections.append(Connection(to: nodeC, cost: 6))
nodeB.connections.append(Connection(to: nodeD, cost: 1))
nodeB.connections.append(Connection(to: nodeE, cost: 3))
nodeC.connections.append(Connection(to: nodeF, cost: 8))
nodeD.connections.append(Connection(to: nodeE, cost: 4))
```

```
nodeE.connections.append(Connection(to: nodeG, cost: 9))
nodeF.connections.append(Connection(to: nodeG, cost: 7))
```

Step 4: Set beginning and destination nodes and call Dijkstra's algorithm to find the shortest path.

```
let sourceNode = nodeA
let destinationNode = nodeG

var path = dijskastraShortestPath(source: sourceNode,
destination: destinationNode)
if let succession: [String] = path?.array.reversed().
compactMap({ $0 as? sampleGraphNode}).map({$0.name}) {
  print("Quickest path: \(succession)")
} else {
  print("No path between \(sourceNode.name) &
  \(destinationNode.name)")
}
```

The output will be

```
Quickest path: ["A", "B", "E", "G"]
```

# Conclusion

In this chapter, you have learned about graph algorithms and strategies behind them. You mastered about breadth-first search, depth-first search, and Dijkstra's algorithms and their advantages and disadvantages. By now you should have a good understanding of how to implement these algorithms and which one to choose based on the requirements.

# CHAPTER 17

# Choosing the Best Algorithm

We have learned different types of algorithms such as sorting, searching, and graph algorithms, and there are likely to be many possible algorithms which perform the same task. The question is, if we want to search for a value in the list, which type of searching algorithm do we have to choose? By analyzing various algorithms, we will study this question in this chapter.

There are many ways of comparing algorithms, but in this chapter, we will focus on time complexity and space complexity.

> Time complexity: Required time for accomplishing the task

> Space complexity: Required memory for accomplishing the task

We will examine the different types of algorithms that we explained in this book.

© Elshad Karimov 2020
E. Karimov, *Data Structures and Algorithms in Swift*,
https://doi.org/10.1007/978-1-4842-5769-2_17

# Sorting Algorithms

We have learned that sorting algorithms order the values in the list from smallest to largest, and there are many sorting algorithms that are available in computer science. To choose the one which perfectly matches our program, we have to possess deep knowledge about how they perform in different situations.

## Bubble Sort

It is very useful when the list is very nearly sorted – if only two elements are out of place. Bubble sort's space requirement is at a minimum because the elements are swapped in place without using additional temporary storage.

| Bubble Sort | Best Case | Worst Case |
|---|---|---|
| Time Complexity | $O(n)$ | $O(n^2)$ |
| Space Complexity | $O(1)$ | $O(1)$ |

## Selection Sort

It is similar to bubble sort that performs well on a small list and its space requirement is at a minimum. The best, average, and worst case time complexity is $O(n^2)$ which is independent of distribution of data.

| Selection Sort | Best Case | Worst Case |
|---|---|---|
| Time Complexity | $O(n^2)$ | $O(n^2)$ |
| Space Complexity | $O(1)$ | $O(1)$ |

# Insertion Sort

It is quite efficient when used on a small array of data. Quadratic runtime $O(n^2)$ can upgrade to a respectable $O(n*k)$, where k is the steps it needs to tread back up the array to swap the previous element with the current one. If the list is partially sorted, it can perform even better than quick sort.

| Insertion Sort | Best Case | Worst Case |
|---|---|---|
| Time Complexity | O(n) | O(n²) |
| Space Complexity | O(1) | O(n) |

# Merge Sort

It is quicker for larger lists because unlike insertion and bubble sort it does not loop through the list. Space complexity is always O(n) as you have to store the elements somewhere. Additional space complexity can be O(n) in an implementation using arrays and O(1) in linked list implementations. In practice implementations using lists need additional space for list pointers, so unless you already have the list in memory, it shouldn't matter.

| Merge Sort | Best Case | Worst Case |
|---|---|---|
| Time Complexity | O(n) (O(n Logn)) | O(n Logn) |
| Space Complexity | O(1) | O(n) |

# Quick Sort

As mentioned before, quick sort uses divide and conquer like merge sort and it is a recursive algorithm. Its worst-case running time is as bad as selection sort and insertion sort. On the other hand, its average-case running time is as good as the merge sort. So the question is, why do we need it when it is at least as good as merge sort? That's because the constant factor hidden in the Big O notation for quick sort is quite good. In practice, quick sort outperforms merge sort, and it significantly outperforms selection sort and insertion sort. The selection of a pivot element plays an important role for quick sort's efficiency.

| Quick Sort | Best Case | Worst Case |
|---|---|---|
| Time Complexity | O(n logn) | O(n²) |
| Space Complexity | O(logn) | O(n) |

# Search Algorithms

Searching algorithms are designed to check for an element or retrieve an element from any data structure where it is stored.

## Linear Search vs. Binary Search

A linear search scans one element at a time and the time for searching keeps increasing as the number of elements are increased.

| Linear Search | Best Case | Worst Case |
|---|---|---|
| Time Complexity | O(1) | O(n) |
| Space Complexity | O(1) | O(1) |

A binary search cuts down the search to half, and based on the middle element, it continues to search either the left or right side of the middle element in the given list.

| Binary Search | Best Case | Worst Case |
|---|---|---|
| Time Complexity | O(1) | O(logn) |
| Space Complexity | O(1) | O(1) |

Differences

- Binary search requires the data to be sorted, but linear search does not.

- Binary search accesses data randomly, whereas linear search accesses data sequentially.

- Binary search performs ordering comparisons, whereas linear search performs equality comparisons.

**A linear search** searching for 7 is shown in Figure 17-1.

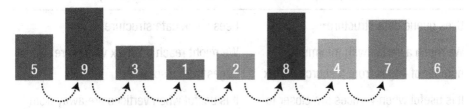

*Figure 17-1.* *Linear search example*

A **binary search** searching for 7 is shown in Figure 17-2.

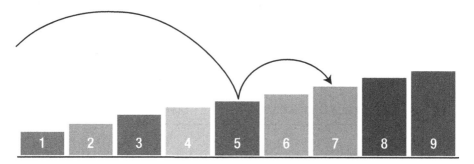

***Figure 17-2.***  *Binary search example*

# Graph Search Algorithms (GSA)

It is obvious that graph search algorithms are used in graph data structures. GSA searches through the nodes of a graph to find our target.

Breadth-First Search (BFS) vs. Depth-First Search (DFS)

| Breadth-First Search (BFS) | Depth-First Search (DFS) |
|---|---|
| Uses queue data structure | Uses stack data structure |
| We reach a vertex with minimum number of edges from a source vertex. | We might reach a vertex with more edges from a source. |
| It is useful when vertices are closer to the given source. | It is useful when vertices are away from the source. |
| It considers neighbors first; this is why it is not suitable for decision-making trees used in games and puzzles. | It is useful for decision-making trees because we make a decision and then explore all paths through this decision. |
| Time complexity is O(V+N), where V stands for vertices and N stands for nodes. | Time complexity is O(V+N), where V stands for vertices and N stands for nodes. |

# Dijkstra's Algorithm

The usage of a priority queue in breadth-first search makes it a Dijkstra's algorithm. With a priority queue, each task added to the queue has a "priority" and will slot in accordingly into the queue based on its priority level. Dijkstra's algorithm should be used when you have no knowledge on the graph and cannot estimate the distance from each node to the target.

# Index

## A

Arrays
    adding element, 5
    element index, 2
    features, 2
    functions and properties
        count, 7
        first and last elements, 7
        isEmpty, 6
        reverse functions, 7
    individual variable declaration, 1
    multidimensional array, 2
    mutating operation, 4
    one-dimensional array, 1
    reallocation, 3
    removing element, 6
    reserve capacity, 3
    retrieve values, 4
    subscript syntax, 8

## B, C

Big O
    add *vs.* multiplication, 128, 129
    amortized time
        elements, 129
        Log N runtimes, 130
        recursive runtimes, 131
    calculate complexity, 126–128
    drop constants/nondominant
        terms, 125, 126
    if-else, 126
    loops, 127
    nested loops, 127
    options, 121
    space complexity, 124–125
    time complexity (*see* Time
        complexity)
Binary Search Tree (BST)
    characteristics, 87
    deleting process
        leaf, 94, 95
        node, 95
        remove function, 96–99
    implementation, 88
    insertion, 89–91
    searching
        process, 88, 92–94
    structure, 87
Binary trees
    balanced tree, 80
    basic structure, 77
    complete tree, 80
    full tree, 78
    implementation, 81
    perfect, 79

© Elshad Karimov 2020
E. Karimov, *Data Structures and Algorithms in Swift*,
https://doi.org/10.1007/978-1-4842-5769-2

# D, E